The Parrot Wizard's Guide to Well-Behaved Parrots 2nd Edition

By Michael Sazhin

Parrot Wizard Inc.
– New York –

While great care has been taken to ensure the accuracy and presentation of the information in this book, every parrot is different and it is up to you to make your own handling decisions. As greater information and experience becomes available, parrot handling techniques may change. Consequently, neither the publisher nor writer can take responsibility if information in whole or in part does not work for your parrot. Please use common sense when applying enclosed advice.

The Parrot Wizard's Guide to Well-Behaved Parrots 2nd Edition
Copyright © 2021 by Parrot Wizard Inc.

All rights reserved. No part of this book may be reproduced or transmitted in any form or by any means without written permission from the author.

With special thanks to Ginger Duplisse, Amy Hopkins, Kristine, Taylor, Dr. Greg Burkett DVM DABVP, Dr. Todd Driggers DVM, and James Kemp for their support and feedback, and an extra special thanks to Marianna Sazhin for her participation and taking great care of our parrots!

For more articles, videos, products, and private consultations:
www.ParrotWizard.com

ISBN 978-0-578-76258-6

Printed in the United States of America
Cover design and artwork by Lu Roli

Table of Contents

Foreword (by Dr. Greg Burkett DVM) 10
Preface 13
Introduction 14
Chapter 1: Getting a Parrot 19
Chapter 2: Situating the Parrot 49
Chapter 3: Early Interactions 62
Chapter 4: Taming & Training 79
Chapter 5: Managing Good Behavior 127
Chapter 6: Flight 152
Chapter 7: Trick Training 176
Chapter 8: Problem Solving 203
Chapter 9: Socialization 240
Chapter 10: Lifestyle 266
Conclusion 279
Glossary 281
On Becoming the Parrot Wizard 287
Photos 290

Appendix A: Further Reading 305
Appendix B: Useful Products 310
Index of Photos & Illustrations 314
Index 316

Dedicated to the companion parrots of the world so that with this knowledge owners and parrots may find a mutually fulfilling relationship.

Detailed Table of Contents

Foreword (by Dr. Greg Burkett DVM) 10
Preface 13
Introduction 14

Chapter 1: Getting a Parrot 19
    Reasons to Get a Parrot 20
    Reasons Not to Get a Parrot 21
    Cost of Owning a Parrot 26
    Parrot Species 29
    Beginner Bird 34
    Finding Out More About Species 36
    Where to Acquire a Parrot 38
    Multiple Parrots 45
    Health 46

Chapter 2: Situating the Parrot 49
    Cages 51
    Things You Need 52
    Toys & Perches 53
    Hazards 54
    Bringing the Parrot Home 57

Chapter 3: Early Interactions 62
    Nutrition & Diet 67
    Treats 69
    Sleep 71
    Desensitization 72
    Baby Parrots 74

Chapter 4: Taming & Training 79
    Training Setup 81
    Training Schedule 84
    Positive Reinforcement 86
    Punishment 87
    Prevention 88
    Motivation 89
    Healthy Feeding 92
    Clicker Conditioning 95
    Target Training 99
    Step Up 104
    Touch/Grab 115
    Toweling 122
    Turning on Back 124

Chapter 5: Managing Good Behavior 127
    Step Up to Come Out of Cage 129
    Putting Parrot Back in Cage 131
    Weighing 132
    Petting 134
    Shouldering 137
    Potty Training 140

Carrier 143

Grooming 146

Out of Cage Time 149

Chapter 6: Flight **152**

Flight Safety 154

Teaching a Parrot to Fly 156

Fun With Flight 161

Harness Training 165

Chapter 7: Trick Training **176**

Basics of Teaching Tricks 177

Cues 181

Target-Based Tricks 183

Cue-Based Tricks 187

Retrieve-Based Tricks 188

Maintaining Tricks 192

Talking 194

Encouraging Parrots to Talk 195

Setting Up Phrases 197

Vocalization Training Devices 198

Capturing Phrases 199

Chapter 8: Problem Solving **203**

Biting 205

Screaming 216

Plucking 220

Hormonal Problems 224

Adolescence 228

    Parrot Bonds to Other Person 231
    Prevention 233
    Flighted Problems 235

Chapter 9: Socialization **240**
    Introducing Objects 242
    Introducing People 246
    Going Outside 255
    Taking Trips 261
    Boarding 263

Chapter 10: Lifestyle **266**
    Toys 267
    Parrot Stands 270
    Tabletop Perch 272
    Training Perch 273
    Window & Shower Perch 274
    Tree Stand... 275

Conclusion **279**
Glossary **281**
On Becoming the Parrot Wizard **287**
Photos **290**

Appendix A: Further Reading **305**
Appendix B: Useful Products **310**
Index of Photos & Illustrations **314**
Index **316**

Foreword By Dr. Greg Burkett, Diplomate ABVP (Avian)

I am Dr. Greg Burkett. I am a veterinarian Board Certified in avian medicine and surgery, and I have been working with birds for nearly 40 years. I have known Michael for several years. I have seen his seminars and performances and I am very impressed.

His skills are unmatched and he is very dedicated to helping people and their parrots. From a veterinary perspective, I find this book to be useful for keeping your bird healthy. A valuable outcome following Michael's techniques is that as an owner you will know how to recognize if your bird is not well because you will be in tune with your bird. It will also teach you how to socialize your bird with people and to train your bird to behave during a visit to your veterinarian. For example, if you follow the teachings of this book it will make it easy to put your bird on a scale to be weighed by your veterinarian. Adopting these methods of training, your bird will be well-behaved, less anxious, and less stressed during the veterinarian exam. As an owner, you too will be less anxious and stressed knowing that your bird is comfortable being handled and examined.

Michael Sazhin is The Parrot Wizard. He is known worldwide for helping parrot owners develop good relationships and form strong bonds with their companion birds.

His interest in birds began at an early age and was fueled by his fascination of flight. His passion for airplanes and the idea of flying led him to become a pilot. Being a pilot affords him the ability to fly to many places to give seminars, perform bird shows, and offer training classes. While he was in college he acquired his first bird; he followed his passion and began developing techniques to teach his birds behaviors that involved their unique ability to fly.

Michael has been traveling around the world to see parrots in the wild. He has visited several continents including Australia, Africa, and South America. Michael enjoys sharing stories of his travels and the information he gathered about wild parrots. He especially enjoys lecturing on the behaviors they exhibit in the wild and how he incorporates natural behaviors into his training techniques. Michael also travels internationally to give seminars and presentations to bird clubs and parrot enthusiasts. Most recently he has visited Prague, Moscow, and Oslo to give presentations and seminars. He has been the headliner at the German National Parrot Conference for the last 5 years and presented at Parrot Palooza for the last 2 years. In addition, in 2018 he received the YouTube Silver Play Button award for reaching 100,000 subscribers. He has even been featured on television on The Late Show with David Letterman, The Steve Harvey Show, America's Got Talent, and others both in America and abroad.

Whether you already own a bird or are planning to get one, this book will be a great reference to help you make your bird the best companion possible. Owning a companion pet bird is one of the most rewarding experiences anyone can have. Not only are they great companions, they provide endless entertainment. They are very intelligent and can learn things very quickly. When owning a pet bird, it is critical that you teach them at least the basic handling commands so they are suitable as pets; good behavior should never be taken for granted. These commands include "up" to a perch or hand, "down" to a perch or hand, "stay", a recall command such as "come", and a command for potty training such as "go poop". There is even more that you should train your bird to do that can have a pet bird behave in desirable ways in order to be good companions. In this book Michael covers all of the important areas of teaching your bird manners, as well as taming techniques and trick training. In addition to the aforementioned, he covers how to properly take your bird out of the cage and how to return them to their cage; how to get them into their carrier; how to manage biting behaviors; and how to properly pet your bird. Parrots are wild birds and have wild instincts. These wild instincts cause natural behaviors that are undesirable in captivity; behaviors that are often troublesome in the home. The idea for taming and training these commands and behaviors is to encourage more desirable behaviors. The techniques covered in this book are very effective at developing good behavior in pet birds thereby making them better pets.

Reading this wonderful book is not enough. You must put in the time and have the patience to incorporate these methods into teaching and training your companion parrot. Doing so will not only benefit your bird, it will benefit you by making your companion parrot a better more enjoyable pet.

Preface

My involvement with parrots started out much like with any other parrot owner. I was looking for a pet, thought a bird might be fun, and got one at a pet shop. I knew nothing about how to handle one and had to learn it all from scratch.

In just a few years I went from someone who wouldn't handle any animals to making TV performances with my parrots. However, it is everything in between that I would like to share that will no doubt be helpful to you.

First and foremost my parrots are my companion pets. I would not be doing any performances or training with them if I thought it was harmful to them in any way. As it turns out, it's the exact opposite and it brings out the best pet qualities in them. I want to share this success with you.

This second edition of the Parrot Wizard's Guide to Well-Behaved Parrots brings you my same parrot keeping methodology for success, but with an upgraded presentation and more information. This version will make it even easier and more clear for you to achieve those magical results with your bird.

My parrots taught me how to be firm but gentle, kind but challenging, deliberate but adaptive, and above all patient. It is my purpose to share with you my parrot owning approach in whole that has led to what I would consider some genuinely well-behaved parrots. May this book help you find the well-behaved parrot in your bird and in yourself!

Introduction

By default, parrots are wild animals and have no need or desire to strike up a relationship with their human. Just because you paid money for your bird in no way convinces it that it should do as you ask. This book is meant to teach you how to approach your parrot and its environment to foster the ideal human-pet relationship. However, none of this is ever at the expense of the bird. All procedures are thoughtfully produced to benefit both human and parrot alike.

My purpose as a parrot owner, and likewise the purpose of this book, is to have a happy, healthy, well-behaved parrot whose companionship I can enjoy and vice versa. What is a well-behaved parrot? Well, this includes not only the things it does but also the things it doesn't do. A well-behaved parrot doesn't bite the owner or other people during normal handling. It steps up whenever asked. A well-behaved parrot steps up to come out of the cage, but it also voluntarily steps up to go back in the cage without any fuss. The well-behaved parrot allows and usually even enjoys petting. The well-behaved parrot rarely or never poops on people, but instead does its business in a designated area. The well-behaved parrot politely asks to come out or gets your attention by talking/vocalizing rather than screaming. It will allow you to grab it and not have much anxiety over vet visits or grooming. The well-behaved parrot can be taken outside (with proper restraining measures) and is well-mannered in public. At home, it recognizes and uses suitable parrot designated perches instead of places it should not go on. Ultimately, within the constraints of nature, the well-behaved parrot is the companion pet that we desire it to be.

The reason it is so important to develop a good behavior system with your parrot as early as possible is not only to protect your sanity, but also to make it possible for you to enjoy your parrot's company. If the parrot does not reliably step up, or bites people, or cannot be handled, you will not get to enjoy the experience you acquired a pet for in the first place. Likewise, the parrot will miss out on your companionship and not even realize how good things can really be. By applying this approach, you will create the blank canvas that you will be able to fill with your own personal relationship with your parrot.

It doesn't matter if you are a first time parrot owner or a long time veteran. Everyone can benefit from this approach. Best of all, it can be applied to any parrot. It doesn't matter if your parrot is big or small, young or old. This is a universal approach that will help you build a relationship with any parrot, because it is based on their very nature.

My approach is centered around health, companionship, and lifestyle. These are vital to the parrot and also highly desirable to us as parrot owners. Without the parrot being in great health, good-behavior is not possible. Many behavioral problems are rooted in poor health or nutrition, thus solving behavior starts with focusing on health. See the *Parrot Wizard Blueprint to Success* on page 304 for a better idea of what my approach is all about.

The flowchart helps tie together the topics covered in this book and how they play a role in developing a well-behaved parrot. This comes from the trifecta of Health, Companionship, and Lifestyle!

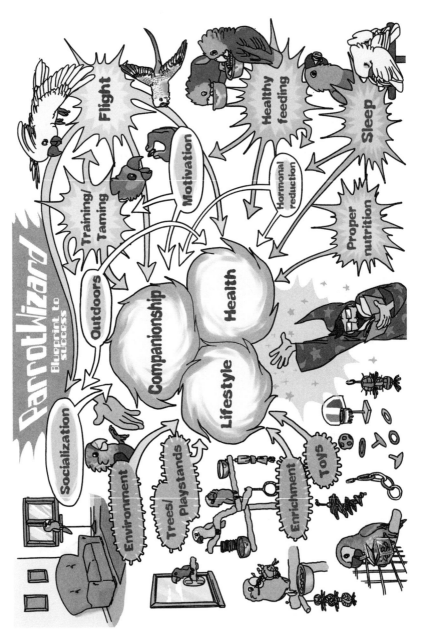

Color version on Page 304

Throughout this book, you will learn how to improve your parrot's health, companionship, and lifestyle in order to bring out the most well-behaved parrot!

Health and companionship go hand in hand. Lifestyle drives health and improves companionship.

Proper diet is essential for a parrot's health and well-being. Sufficient sleep is required for a parrot's health. It also prevents hormonal triggers by keeping a consistent daylight schedule. Healthy feeding also reduces hormonal triggers and is there for training motivation. A motivated parrot is more likely to behave as a good companion than one that does whatever it wants. Motivation allows the parrot to be tamed and trained which greatly shapes its desirability as a companion. Furthermore, training allows you to manage the parrot's flight ability and take it outdoors. Outdoor natural sunshine is necessary for a parrot's health and going outside is a great way to socialize a parrot. Flight makes for a more social parrot because it has the confidence to approach or flee but this also makes it a better companion by not biting. The flighted parrot can be a better companion because it can come to you of its own will. Flight is also the best form of exercise for keeping a parrot healthy.

Setting up an effective environment for your bird will help adapt the parrot from forest life to home life. Trees and play stands can be used to encourage good behavior and keep the parrot engaged. Enrichment improves behavior both inside and outside of the cage. Likewise, bird toys will encourage a parrot to spend its destructive energy on something expendable and safe. As you see, the combination of all of these elements develops a well-behaved parrot.

I'm not going to say that I can guarantee you will achieve all of this right away. As the saying goes, Rome wasn't built in a day. Parrots are undomesticated wild birds, so accomplishing good companion pet parrot behavior can take time and effort. However, if you keep working little by little toward these goals, ultimately you will look back and realize that you've come ever so far. You will be pleased with your parrot, and in this process your parrot will also develop a relationship with you. You will mold your parrot's preferences and encourage it to want appropriate things (for example, to play with toys rather than with moldings). As you follow procedures in this book to make yourself more acceptable to the parrot, ultimately you will have a parrot that is far more acceptable to you as well! It's a two-way relationship and what you give is what you receive. The goal here is to keep this process fun, safe, and immensely rewarding both for you and your parrot. *It's not magic, it's an educated, effective, heartfelt approach.*

Chapter 1: Getting a Parrot

Having a parrot can bring you a lot of thrill and amusement. It can also be one of the most challenging kinds of pet ownership you have ever encountered. Parrots are highly intelligent, social, complex, aggressive, cuddly, and among the most misunderstood of all common pets. *They can talk, they can fly, but can bite 'til you cry*. With a lot of dedication, time, patience, and some help from this book you should be able to achieve a loving, mutual relationship with your parrot.

If you bought this book then you probably already own a parrot or are contemplating acquiring one. If you are thinking of getting a parrot, this chapter will help you decide whether or not a parrot is right for you. If you already have a parrot, it may help you decide whether or not to get another parrot. In either case, it will help you decide whether to get a parrot or not and what kind is right for you.

Reasons to Get a Parrot

There are many reasons that people get parrots. They are amusing to watch, sometimes able to talk. They are beautiful to look at, amazing in flight, and quite an exotic pet. In order to get a parrot, any species of parrot, you must want or be prepared for all of the following:

-A bird
-A pet with high intelligence
-A noise maker
-Longevity
-Complexity
-A project to work on

-A perpetual child

-A being that takes but doesn't necessarily give back

You must realize that a parrot is the most intelligent animal you can own as a pet and be prepared for the challenge. Also, you have to desire this challenge. If owning parrots were simple, you wouldn't need this entire manual on how to get them to behave the way you want.

Parrots really are not suitable pets for most people. They just aren't a ready-to-go pet like a domesticated animal. But for a select few, they can be the most amazing pet you can have. They move in three dimensions, they make entertaining vocalizations, and watching them play and interact is astounding. You have to earn their trust and work with them every day for their entire lives. To some people, these qualities are actually desirable and a parrot is the pet they seek. Genuine parrot lovers choose to have parrots because they love the challenge that they bring and not because they want something easy to take care of.

Reasons Not to Get a Parrot

The reasons not to get a parrot are far more extensive than the reasons to get one. I have consulted all too many people who really didn't want what owning a parrot actually turned out to be. These people were unfortunately misled by the pretty colors, docile baby qualities, pet stores, or other parrot owners into thinking that a parrot is like a puppy. Unfortunately this couldn't be further from the truth. Parrots are entirely wild animals (hand fed or not) and will treat your home as though it's the middle of the jungle. Parrots have no domestication nor innate reason to love you, listen to you, or behave in a way you would like. Just because you bought the parrot, provide food, clean its cage, buy toys, and spoil it, these are not reasons for it to reciprocate anything to you. This is a difficult concept for people to come to terms with, but essentially, a parrot is like a little child and has much to take and little to give back. If you must have an animal that will love you just because, you are really much better off with a dog.

Parrots are extremely messy animals. In the forest they simply sit on a tree branch and poop over the edge, drop their food, and make a mess and it's not their problem. In the home, this is an undesirable quality but one you must come to terms with. A lot of cleaning will be necessary. And, even though the bird lives in a cage, it does not mean the mess won't spread far beyond.

Price also should not play a major role in the purchase of a parrot whether it's a parakeet or a macaw. Just because the bird is $40, $4000, or free should not play a role in the seriousness of the decision involved. It is still a valuable life that will be entirely dependent on you for survival but with no awareness of this or gratitude in the process. In terms of cost, it is important to realize that the long term costs of owning a parrot far outweigh the price of purchasing one.

The colorful appearance of parrots ought not to be a major deciding factor either. It won't be long before you grow used to the appearance, yet the personality and behavior will persist forever. Some parrots end up plucking their feathers out. Then their original appearance gets lost, so it is important that you enjoy the personality foremost. The illusion of the parrot's baby personality must also not drive the decision. Baby parrots can often be held, cuddled, and handled effortlessly, but this is no indication that they will remain this way into adulthood. You must realize that even the most easy-going baby parrot will still require extensive training to remain that way as an adult or it will likely revert to being a wild and difficult bird.

Realize that parrots are birds and birds fly. This is a fact overlooked all too much because of the illusion that wing clipping creates. In reality, everything about a parrot is geared for flight and their "flightedness" is a fundamental part of them. Many people don't want to have a flying parrot in their home so they clip the wings. However, this often leads to behavioral problems that are even more difficult to solve than managing to live with a flighted bird in the first place. It is best to realize that parrots are born to fly and either accept that or choose a different pet. Clipping wings is not only a cruel and unnecessary practice, but it is also a poor substitute for effective parrot keeping.

The desirable talking qualities that parrots are known to have are also one of their greatest draw backs. With the ability to imitate voices also comes the ability to imitate the most annoying of noises. Parrots pick up on the bad sounds with even more vigor than the desirable ones. For every cute phrase that a parrot learns to say, it will often have an extensive repertoire of annoying sounds to bombard you with. It could be the sound of the smoke detector, the neighbor's dog barking, coughing, yelling, or whatever noise that gets under your skin. The talking quickly gets old but the noise making and screaming persist for a lifetime. You may get tired of the parrot talking, but the parrot never will. It will spend minutes to hours of the day making a lot of noise, and this is something you will have to contend with. It is their natural instinct to do this. No amount of training can eliminate it entirely, however, we can try to manage the amount relative to the species.

Parrots are also some of the most vicious biters for their size. Sharp, powerful beaks coupled with natural defensive aggression are a recipe for disaster as a pet. There are a multitude of different reasons that parrots may bite and as an owner you have to learn to deal with all of these kinds. You cannot just pay money for a parrot and then expect it "not to bite the hand that feeds it." They will bite the hand that feeds without a second thought. Parrots don't bite with the intent of eating other animals as a carnivore would, instead they bite to communicate. Sometimes they bite to drive others away, other times they bite because they are jealous, because they are scared, because they want attention, or sometimes just to get a scratch. The untrained parrot makes its point known only with its beak. The advice in this book is meant to help you change this and make the relationship manageable. But you must realize what a difficult animal you are getting involved with and that following the steps outlined in these chapters is essential. It is a relationship you will have to earn and there is no shortcut around it.

Yet another reason not to acquire a parrot is merely out of pity. Never buy a bird just because it is being sold in terrible conditions, a rescue in need of a home, or because someone offered it to you for free. It is often the good intentions of owners that show pity to such birds that others take advantage of and intentionally neglect/abuse them. There is nothing wrong with rescuing a parrot but it must happen with full awareness of what you are getting yourself into and not merely out of pity.

The long lifespan of parrots (20-40 years for smaller and 50-100 years for larger) is not necessarily a good thing. With such a long lifespan comes a phenomenal commitment! Think about your age and then how old you will be at the life expectancy of the parrot. So much will change in this span of time. You must be prepared to adjust your life as you go to accommodate for your flying companion and not just get rid of it. Rehoming a parrot often carries major psychological/health implications for the bird and also fills rescues beyond capacity. The lifespan of parrots is so long that there already aren't enough homes for all the unwanted ones. Basically there are far more being raised than dying of old age, so the number only keeps growing. Adding more unwanted parrots to this means a poorer life for all abandoned parrots. The only way to avoid this is to make an absolute commitment to keeping the bird for life by understanding the full ramifications of the decision.

Parrots are a terrible pet for children and should never be regarded as a children's pet. They bite, scream, and live for a long time, none of which are good traits for teaching a youngster about responsibility. These are not an animal for a child to grow up with and that's it. Even a cockatiel bought for a 10 year old will likely live until that child is 30! So much will change in those years that would be impossible to foresee. But, the biggest reason not to get a parrot for a child is because they are difficult animals and will bite. It may take years of dedicated taming and training before a parrot can easily be handled by others. Children will quickly grow bored and disappointed when they realize a parrot doesn't just repeat anything they say and is impossible to just play with.

If you don't already have a parrot, I really hope you can read this entire book and do more research before making a decision that will impact your life and the life of another being for many years to come. My goal is not to persuade you not to get a parrot. It is to help you realize if a parrot is not a suitable pet for you or to reinforce that it really is what you want. I am trying to save you the burden of having an extremely difficult animal to take care of and having to follow all the advice in this book. With full awareness of the commitment involved, I think you are best equipped to make a responsible decision.

Cost of Owning a Parrot

When contemplating the acquisition of a parrot, it is very important to consider your budget as birds can be very costly to keep. The cost of the bird itself is negligible compared to the long term cost of ownership, so don't let the price tag drive your decision. If you think a certain species is barely affordable, realize that the cost of upkeep may be outside your budget entirely.

Parrots are highly destructive creatures and require endless supplies of perches and toys to keep them occupied. They consume specialized diets, require expensive vet care, and even require many costly alterations to your household environment for their safe keeping. It is inevitable that you will need to spend a lot of money buying additional things for your parrot like a tree, stands, carrier, harness, air purifier, and countless other items you may not have originally thought of.

All of these things are a necessary part of achieving a well-behaved parrot. Without the aid of these things, it will be difficult to divert noisy, destructive, flighty behavior that is innate to these birds. Believe me, it is still cheaper to go through countless toys than to have your furniture, moldings, and personal possessions destroyed.

A general formula I have devised for ballparking the yearly and lifetime cost of owning a parrot generally correlates to the store retail price of the parrot species. If you are adopting, rescuing, or accepting a bird from a friend, that price obviously won't reflect what I am describing. Instead consider the price of that species if it were bought at a store. The formula goes like this. Where P is the retail price of that kind of parrot, you can expect to spend 2P on the day of purchase and then 1P every year thereafter including the first year. Let me break this down. When you buy a parrot, you will also have to buy a cage (which typically costs 1/2P), some perches, food, and toys just to get you started. Thus, you will spend the amount the parrot costs on the parrot itself and that much more on the initial set of supplies. Then, you will spend the same amount the parrot cost every year on consumable items such as food, toys, perches, other supplies, and specialized avian vet check ups. In the first year, be prepared to spend 3P-4P because after the initial purchase you will realize all the additional things that will be helpful (such as cleaning supplies, replacing all Teflon cookware and appliances, carrier, harness, tree, etc). This can be a very large sum. For a $1000 parrot, you will easily end up spending $3000-$4000 in the first year and a $1000 every year thereafter. When you consider that this parrot will likely live 50 years, that's $50,000 you can expect to spend in its lifetime (in current dollars without adjustment for inflation). For this reason I suggest that it is imperative to think beyond just the purchase price of the bird.

  The reason this formula correlates for most parrots is because the larger ones tend to be more expensive and likewise they require bigger accommodations and more supplies. The formula doesn't work for budgies because they are extremely underpriced, so consider them more along the lines of the same cost to keep as a cockatiel. On the other hand, extra exotic species may not be substantially more to keep than comparatively sized ones that are cheaper. In those cases make calculations based on the more typical species. African grey parrots are also disproportionately priced and their upkeep cost will be less than the purchase cost.

While it is possible to cut corners and spend less, the goal is to achieve a well-behaved parrot and unfortunately that comes with a price. Great supplies, nutritious food, and the best veterinary care are necessary for keeping your parrot happy and healthy. You cannot even begin to expect a parrot to be well-behaved without it being healthy and happy foremost.

For these reasons, consider and budget for the recurring costs of ownership and don't dwell too much on the initial cost of acquiring the parrot. If you are getting a parrot at a reduced price or even for free, don't let that initial cost affect your decision. Consider the long term costs because they are the same for parrots of a comparable size regardless of the initial acquisition cost.

Parrot Species

Dogs come in breeds. Parrots come in species. In fact the most distantly related parrots are taxonomically as distant as cats are to dogs! This is an important thing to realize when choosing a species because the behavioral differences can be quite substantial even though we call all of them parrots.

Parrots come in all shapes and sizes from different continents of the world. Although the training techniques are fairly universal, the innate behavior you will experience from different species will vary drastically. It becomes more essential to choose a parrot for unfavorable traits you can tolerate than for the favorable ones you desire. People can tolerate or even develop new things they enjoy with a parrot that is lacking on the favorable. However, perpetually putting up with unbearable traits for many years becomes too much for many people and they end up relinquishing their parrots to rescues. It is important to set the relationship up for success from the start by choosing a species that will suit you well before even applying the concepts you are about to learn. No matter how suitable a fit a certain species may be, it will still be inevitable to have to do a lot of other things to tame the wild out of the bird. However, there are many innate characteristics you can never change so it is important to avoid species that are prone to them rather than regret it later.

It is important to understand that the generalizations presented here and by others are just that, generalizations. Each bird is an individual so there is a lot more to it. However, if the generalizations of a certain species are unfavorable to you, it would not be wise taking a chance acquiring it in hope that the specific individual doesn't live up to to those generalizations. Likewise, when acquiring an individual of a certain species whose characteristics you look upon favorably, be prepared that your individual may not express any of them. In other words, not all African greys talk, not all cockatoos pluck, and not all conures scream. Generalizations are just a means to help you assess the criteria by which to choose. At that point you are committed to making it work whether the bird lives up to those general traits or not.

The major categories of parrots available in aviculture are parakeets, cockatiels, parrotlets, lovebirds, Amazons, cockatoos, conures, macaws, lories, Poicephalus, African greys, caiques, and eclectus. Some of these categories are specific species, others are genera, while others are entire families or just birds sharing a common trait. However, since these are categories that are commonly used in parrot lingo, it is best to analyze them without getting too much into the accurate nomenclature.

Parakeets are small long-tailed parrots. There are many species but the most common ones you may encounter include budgerigars, ring-necks, Alexandrine, and monk parakeets (Quaker parrots). Size of parakeets will range a fair amount but never be anything more than what you can keep on your hand. They all have beautifully long tails and are good fliers. They tend to be poor talkers, shrill, and less people-friendly. However, they are usually easier to take care of, less expensive to keep, more forgiving, and simpler to train. Avoid any color mutations except the standard wild color. The specially colored ones may look exotic, but they are often very inbred for color, are prone to illness, and usually have less desirable personalities.

Cockatiels are the smallest and most distinct of all cockatoos. They are a fairly small bird with a movable crest on the head. They are in many ways one of the best parrots for a complete beginner. Cockatiels don't really talk, but they can develop an ability to whistle tunes. The cage size and space requirements are small enough that they can be kept in virtually any size dwelling. Likewise, they are good fliers and can get by even in smaller rooms. They are quick learners and easier to get along with. Their movable crest signals their mood and makes their body language very easy to learn and read, even for first time owners.

Parrotlets and lovebirds are small in size but big in presence. They are feisty birds with a lot of attitude. This does not mean they cannot be tamed, but don't let their small size mislead you into thinking they are easy. In terms of price, parrotlets and lovebirds can cost nearly as much as some of the larger small parrots. They won't be as loud as a large parrot but they can still produce very audible shrieks and calls. If you are tight on space but not on budget and are looking for the personality of larger parrots, parrotlets and lovebirds may suit the role well.

Conures are adored for their colors and playfulness. On the other hand, they can be quite noisy for a smaller parrot and bitey as well. Green-cheeked conures are some of the smallest conures available in aviculture. In a body barely bigger than a budgerigar, they pack a lot of attitude and are favored by people who cannot keep larger parrots. Sun conures are the most colorful. Yet, they can be some of the most shrill and noisiest. There is another handful of species of different sizes and colors available in between.

The Poicephalus genus includes seven species that are available in aviculture that share many similar traits. Their sizes and colors vary somewhat, but their personalities are more alike. They tend to be shier and quieter than most other parrots of comparable size. Poicephalus parrots are not known to be good talkers, though there are some exceptions. They are less colorful and tend to be more green or black; however, they are best known as "personality" birds. Poicephalus parrots have the potential of developing a stronger bond and relationship with their human. However, there is also a downside to this in that they can become terribly aggressive towards those they don't like. Senegal parrots are the most common of the Poicephalus.

Caiques stand in a category of their own. There are two species: the black capped and the white bellied. They are a blend of conure and Poicephalus traits in that they are colorful, love to show off, but can also be fairly aggressive. They are best known for their spunk and are not recommended for an owner that likes tranquility.

The Amazon genus spans a vast array of species, yet most of them tend to be of a medium size and green in color. Most Amazons are distinguished mainly by the plumage on their heads. Amazon parrots are typically exquisite talkers and have even been taught to sing. However, when they hit maturity they are also known to be extremely aggressive and can deliver a big bite. They are not well suited for people that can't handle a lot of aggressive testing.

African grey parrots belong to a single genus and two species: the Congo African grey (CAG) and Timneh African grey (TAG). The TAG are smaller in size and have a maroon colored tail while the CAG are larger with a bright red tail. Greys are known to be some of the smartest and best talking parrots. But, don't for a second think that this is necessarily a good thing. They are so intelligent that they are difficult to handle and train. Furthermore, if left unchallenged, this intelligence can turn them to neurotic behavior such as plucking, biting, or screaming. African grey parrots should not be bought merely for their talking ability, they really must be given a home by someone who is genuinely looking for a difficult lifelong challenge.

Cockatoos are easily recognized by the raisable crest on their heads. Most cockatoos are white but there are a few of alternate colors. They are some of the cuddliest and attention seeking of all birds. However, they are also some of the most problematic parrots to own. Their positive traits are easily outweighed by the problems involved with keeping them. They usually are extremely noisy and attention seeking. If they do not receive the excessive amount of attention they desire, they are very likely to revert to plucking, biting, and screaming. Adult male cockatoos can develop major territorial aggression and even deliberately attack people.

Macaws are the biggest parrots and likewise carry big requirements. These parrots are so big that an entire room or aviary is necessary to provide enough space. They are majestic creatures, potentially friendly, extremely loud, and OK talkers. But with such a big bird comes an even bigger responsibility. They have enormous space requirements as well as needs for toys and things to break. It takes an extra layer of dedication to share your home with them.

Beginner Bird

What bird should you start out with? Should you get an easy bird to begin with and then move onto something more challenging? This is very much a personal question, but I do not believe that it is necessary to think this way.

First of all, there is no such thing as a "beginner bird." All parrots, small or large, pose their own unique set of challenges. No matter how small, no parrot is an easy domesticated animal. Even a tiny budgie or parrotlet will require the same taming, training, environment, and persistent effort to develop into a well-behaved pet as a big parrot. Of course the size will be different, the budget will be different, but in principle, things will much be the same.

If you get a small parrot when you really desire a big parrot, what will happen to the small parrot when eventually you get the big parrot of your dreams anyway? Small parrots still live a long time and require much care and attention.

I don't believe that some parrots are necessarily "easier" than others. Typically what makes an "easy" parrot is that it costs less to buy, costs less to keep, and is less capable of delivering a strong bite when you make mistakes in how you treat it. By following the Parrot Wizard methodology, you should not be receiving bites from any parrot, big or small.

The biggest difference in learning and behavior from small to large parrots is the pace. The smaller the parrot, the faster their internal clock is compared to ours. They move faster, think faster, and learn faster. Bigger parrots move slower and at a pace more comparable to our own. This also makes the bigger parrots easier to observe and predict. So, what is easier? The small parrot that learns quickly but also moves more quickly or the large parrot? This really comes down to your personal preference.

Keep in mind that what may be an easy bird for one person may be a difficult one for another. A large parrot might be easy in a large house with a vacant room, but very difficult in a tiny studio. A small energetic parrot may be thrilling for one owner but a disaster flying around and buzzing for another. A noisy parrot may be easy for one person who is tolerant of noise but very difficult for another. It is all about finding personal compatibility rather than labeling an inexpensive or smaller bird as easy.

Now just because there is no such thing as a "beginner bird," does not mean there aren't some birds that beginners should avoid! There are some species that are more noisy or aggressive than someone without experience may be ready to handle. Some individual birds with a history of aggression, health problems, self-mutilation, or neglect may be more than you can handle as a first bird.

For these reasons, I believe that it is best to get the species that is most suitable for you for the long run than to start with a "beginner bird." Get more education and supplies to help you do things right with the right bird for you. Choose the species that is most suitable for your home, lifestyle, preference, and budget and let the Parrot Wizard help you make that become your successful dream bird.

Finding Out More About Species

This brief overview of species is meant to serve strictly as a baseline introduction to the kinds of parrots you might consider. This is by no means sufficient to base a buying decision on. Parrots live for many years (20-80) so the decision you make now will continue to play a role in your life decades from now. There are many resources to make use of to aid your purchasing decision and I suggest you use as many of them as possible.

Books and the internet have a wealth of information about parrot keeping and descriptions of each species. Start by reading general descriptions on the internet. Look at discussions of each species you are interested in on parrot forums (www.TheParrotForum.com is the one I started). Try to talk to owners of specific species and get their perspectives. Don't just ask about the nice aspects of each species but also consider the difficulties. When you have narrowed your search to a few species or genera, you should buy and read a book for each that is available. Find out if there is a local parrot club in your area because meeting other parrot owners and their birds in person can prove extremely informative as well.

The best place to introduce yourself to parrots in person is not at a store or breeder but rather at a parrot rescue. It's easy to see a parrot on TV or in a store and think you want one. It is a whole other story after you see the reality of what they are really like. The baby parrots that can be seen in stores really don't represent what they will be like in adulthood. Since the baby stage lasts a mere three months to three years, the adult form which can last from 19-100 years is far more important to take into consideration. Unlike stores, rescues cannot and usually don't desire to hide reality from you. In a rescue you will really get to see the bad as well as the good sides to each parrot species. I will later urge you to consider adopting a rescue parrot and describe the reasons to you, however, even if you have the full intention of buying from a store or breeder, I still think that you cannot learn more about a parrot species than from a rescue.

I would strongly urge you to volunteer at a parrot rescue (or if not available then at a store) taking care of parrots prior to ever purchasing one. Most people who purchase parrots don't know what it will be like until they get the bird and end up learning along the way. The problem with this is, sometimes they don't realize they don't really want a parrot until after they've already acquired one. If you spend a good amount of time around a rescue, not only will you get to feel the difficulty of ownership, you will also get to practice your parrot handling skills. By getting comfortable around birds before you get yours, you will have a higher likelihood of handling the bird correctly from the very start. This will reduce the probability of doing things incorrectly or invoking behavioral problems out of inexperience. The pre-purchase hands-on practice is exceptionally valuable.

Even if you acquire your parrot from a breeder or rescue, it is still a good idea to visit a bird store. I just don't recommend this as your first impression because pet store staff will surely sugar coat things. It's easy to get carried away at a store and believe that parrots are harmless little angels that make the best pets in the world. But this is very misleading. If you first experience parrots in their reality, you will have a better chance at resisting the temptation of making an uneducated impulse purchase at a store. The benefit of visiting a store with this in mind, however, is that you may get to experience species that you would never see at a rescue or learn about some useful pet supply products. Another great reason to visit a bird store before you acquire a parrot anywhere, is to get a better idea of the supplies and prices you should expect. You may purchase your supplies in store or online, but as a first time owner it is still good to at least familiarize yourself with these things in person.

Where to Acquire a Parrot

Once you have completed your extensive research of parrots and their care and are finally prepared to acquire one, the last question is where? The existing options are from a general pet store, dedicated bird store, parrot breeder, rescue, directly from an owner, or in some cases from the wild. In case you live in a place where the sale of wild captured parrots is still permitted, I strongly urge you not to consider this option if not for humane reasons, then because a wild caught parrot is unlikely to make a good companion house parrot. Also avoid buying a parrot from a general pet store. They often buy their birds in bulk from large mills that tend to take poor care of their birds and the lack of specialization from the store will result in an inferior purchase.

This leaves a bird store, parrot breeder, rescue, or directly from a prior owner as your real options. No matter which of these options you end up choosing, the quality of your companionship will depend far more on what you do (and the advice of this book ought to help guide you in this process) than where you acquired the parrot. Once we've ruled out the unacceptable options, the remainder are all viable except some may be more preferable than the others.

The least favorable of the "acceptable" options is to acquire the parrot directly from a prior owner. The problem with getting the parrot from someone who is selling or giving away their own bird is that they are probably the worst possible source of information. Although on occasion, perfectly well-behaved parrots may be rehomed out of necessity (for example the owner passed away), the majority of people giving away or selling their pet are just fed up with the animal. If you purchase or even take a bird for free from them, you are very likely accepting a poorly behaved parrot that has been poorly cared for. Furthermore, you can't rely on the previous owner for information or further support. You can't take advice from them on how to care for the parrot because they likely failed (which led them to get rid of the bird). Likewise, you can't necessarily trust their stated motives in rehoming the parrot. In order to ensure that it gets another home or fetches a better price, they may sugar coat things or hide problems that you will not realize until it is too late. Oftentimes birds that are sold this way end up being passed around from home to home because of this mess. If you are more experienced and would like to take on a known project, or you are absolutely certain you can trust the source (like a relative or friend), then accepting the parrot from another individual may be right for you. But for a first time owner, I encourage you to seek a parrot from a more informative source.

The next best option is to acquire a baby parrot directly from a reputable bird store. The good news is that you will be able to receive some additional personal support in the future and you get a clean start with a young bird. The disadvantages are that store sold birds aren't raised in optimal conditions, are virtually always clipped, and that store employees are unfamiliar or dishonest about adulthood problems that you will have to face with a parrot. Some advice you get from stores may be good but other advice may be biased.

The biggest advantage of getting a parrot from a bird store is availability. The birds are likely available immediately or some time in the near future. Also, stores are likely to be closer and more local. Breeders tend to be spread farther apart and mostly located in the warmer states.

One advantage of getting a parrot at a store rather than a breeder is that store birds tend to be better socialized to many people. They are usually exposed to a greater number of different people and experiences. On the other hand, there is no guarantee that the handling they have received from other people prior to your purchase was done properly and it could in turn backfire and cause trouble too.

The best way to buy a baby parrot is from a good breeder. I reiterate that it must be a "good" breeder because many do a poor job raising parrots. Unless the parrot is raised by a good breeder, there are plenty of preventable problems you may end up running into. The trouble with finding a good breeder for a first time parrot owner is figuring out what makes a good breeder. The number of years they have been in business, the size or cleanliness of their facility (unless abysmal), or how nice they are to you is practically irrelevant. Much more important considerations are the breeding stock they use, health of parent birds, how they pair their breeding pairs, at what age they pull the babies, what kind of diet they wean them on, whether or not they actively handle the parrots, and whether they clip the parrot's wings.

You definitely want to make sure the breeder weans baby parrots onto a pellet diet. Even though you can potentially change the diet over yourself, this will be difficult and permanently ingrained in the parrot's mind as the food it grew up with. It is difficult to say at which age breeders should pull chicks, but it seems that a reasonable consensus is that it should not be prior to hatching and not later than one month. Whether it is better to pull at one week or three is still up for much debate, but it is well known that pulling too late or too early can pose problems. Usually it is preferable that the breeding stock be comprised of pre-import-ban wild caught pairs because they have stronger genetics (unlike extensively inbred domestic pairs). Otherwise it is important that a domestic breeding pair has been selected on behavior not less than for plumage. A vicious domestic breeding pair may be indicative of the chicks they will produce.

One last essential consideration is whether the breeder fledges all of their chicks and is willing to sell a parrot without clipping its wings. If the breeder clips the birds' wings before they ever fly, don't remotely consider this breeder under any circumstance (even if you are absolutely set on getting a clipped parrot). Not only is this terrible for the parrots' upbringing, but it also demonstrates a degree of incompetence on the part of the breeder to what parrots are really like. If the breeder cannot understand the importance of fledging for the physical and psychological development of young parrots, then you can be certain there are plenty of other things that will be addressed inadequately. Ideally, you should purchase a parrot that is not clipped (please read this entire book and particularly chapter 6 to aid you in this consideration). You will realize that keeping a clipped parrot safe is equally as demanding as keeping a flighted one safe. Yet, it is actually easier to ensure good behavior in a flighted parrot than it is in a clipped one. Many common parrot problems are the direct result of clipping the wings so avoiding this from the very start is ideal. Fledglings that are learning to fly can and will crash into things as they learn, but their bones are soft and they are built to handle this. It is much worse to have a baby parrot clipped and not learn to fly until it is an adult, because then it will get more hurt in the process and have a tougher time learning.

Purchasing a parrot as a baby from a breeder has the advantage of a clean slate, but it also puts a much larger burden on you to raise it perfectly. As a first time owner, you will inevitably be learning on the job. Every mistake you make in the first few weeks and months will end up playing a much more drastic role because it represents a large percent of the parrot's entire life. Also, you can't be sure how the parrot will turn out as an adult. For these reasons, the path to parrot acquisition that I most highly recommend is to adopt your parrot from a good rescue.

Believe it or not, there are actually advantages of acquiring a parrot from a parrot rescue. The biggest one is that what you see is what you get. Some things may still change as the bird is situated and surely you can resolve some problematic behavior, but you will have a realistic overall impression of what the parrot is like. Baby parrots from stores or breeders often give a false impression of tameness that is entirely the result of their young naive age and not the way they will turn out.

I am not suggesting going to a parrot rescue and taking on a vicious, plucker, or screamer parrot as your first parrot. Quite often, rescues will offer perfectly nice companion parrots that were relinquished for one silly reason or another (like moving to a new house, getting bored of having a pet, etc). Since rescues deal with a large number of parrots, they are more likely to come across an easier going parrot to provide to you, knowing that you are a beginner.

Since rescues predominantly deal with adult parrots, they are more likely to be able to provide you long term advice on living with an adult parrot than the short term advice stores give about babies. Another potential advantage of adopting a rescue parrot is that it will already be older. If you are older than 50 years old, buying a baby parrot that can live more than 50 years will create a difficult situation for the parrot when it outlives you. But if you adopt a parrot that has already lived a portion of its life expectancy, this can be an advantage.

Adopting a parrot also has an advantage if you are looking for a parrot that talks. Since baby parrots don't normally demonstrate talking ability until they become older, when you buy a baby you have no idea if that individual will ever become a talker or not. Even the most talkative of parrot species yield non-talking individuals. If you adopt a parrot that is already a good talker, then you have good assurance that it will continue to say the cute phrases it knows and learn new ones from you.

When you visit a parrot rescue, you may come across a parrot that likes you right off the bat! Perhaps you remind it of its previous owner or it may just be love at first sight. Regardless of the reason, you and the facilitators at the rescue will know that this parrot chose you. This can be as much if not more of an advantage than purchasing a baby parrot. Many baby parrots are easy going toward everyone they come across, yet this is destined to change when they hit adolescence. With a baby parrot, there is a greater risk of it switching its allegiance with time. Meanwhile, if you have a great connection with an adult parrot, it will carry a greater chance of remaining this way over time (though nothing is ever completely guaranteed).

Some points of caution when it comes to rescues: don't let rescues convince you that clipping wings is necessary. Rescues are packed with birds and are unable to keep them flighted in limited space. Furthermore, rescues often take in parrots that flew out of people's homes due to owner negligence, so they are naturally preset against flighted parrots. But since you are taking the time to inform yourself about responsible parrot ownership, this does not need to apply to you. Surely the parrot will be clipped upon adoption; however, you should be freely able to allow the parrot's wings to grow back and become flighted over time. If the rescue has a strict clipping policy that will prohibit you from adopting a parrot to keep flighted from them, I urge you to find a more lenient rescue to approach instead.

During the rescue adoption process, you may have to submit to a house visit/inspection by the rescue. Although this may seem a bit intrusive, it is done in the best interest of the parrot. Also, you can assume that the parrots are cared for as well as possible if the rescue takes this much initiative. If a rescue deems you ineligible to adopt a parrot, take this as a credible warning sign that perhaps a parrot would not be suited to live in your household. On the flipside, if you are accepted for adoption, this should help give you confidence for the long road ahead.

Generally, getting a parrot from a store will be quickest, while there may be a waiting period until next breeding season with a breeder. Policies at rescues will vary, with some requiring a waiting period and some being available right away. In either case, I advise patience in finding the optimal bird for you. They live such a long time that a few extra months in finding the best bird for you will be dwarfed by years of enjoyment.

Multiple Parrots

Although some people keep more than one parrot, it is not advisable for the first time parrot owner. For more experienced owners looking to add another bird, there are two ways multiple parrots could be kept: in the same cage (most likely of the same species) as bonded parrots, or in separate cages (especially if they are of different species). For the purpose of attaining well-behaved companion parrots, keeping two in a cage is entirely inadvisable. The birds will likely bond, breed, or fight and in any case, want less to do with the owner.

If you are looking to add an additional but separately kept parrot, there are some essential things to keep in mind. First of all, do not add another parrot until the relationship you have with your first (or all current ones) is an outstanding one. Not only does owning additional parrots involve more work, it also creates an imbalance in the relationship. If the reason you seek an additional parrot is because there is something lacking with the one you already have, getting another bird will not solve this. Instead, use the information in this guide to work on building a stronger relationship with your existing bird. Only after this relationship has been achieved, if you so happen to desire to have another parrot, then you may look into it. Just keep in mind that there is no guarantee that multiple parrots will get along or that relationships won't be strained.

Health

Birds are naturally very rugged healthy animals. They tend not to get sick and if they do, they show little signs of illness. But if/when they do become sick or injured, the outcome is often catastrophic. For these reasons, it is important to build a relationship with an avian veterinarian from the very beginning. It's a great idea to have an avian vet on hand at or before the time you acquire your first parrot.

Whether you adopt, rescue, or buy a baby parrot, it's a very good idea to take it to an avian veterinarian very early on. First of all it creates a relationship between you and your vet. This will allow your vet to get to know the bird from the earliest stage, take some baseline numbers, and let you know if everything is alright.

If you get a parrot from a store or breeder, inquire about the health guarantee. Oftentimes, they require you to take the bird to an avian vet within a short time of purchase.

Make sure to only use an avian vet. Most cat/dog or general veterinarians are not aware of the complex intricacies involved in bird care.

If you are adding an additional parrot to your household, be sure to quarantine it for a minimum of 30 days from your existing flock. This means you should do your best to keep the birds as far apart as possible in your home, wash hands between handling birds, don't take them out together, etc. You could end up infecting your existing birds from the newcomer if you do not observe such quarantine. Don't underestimate the importance of a proper quarantine because many signs of illness take time to develop. Better safe than sorry.

Chapter 1 Checklist:

☐ I want a bird
☐ I don't mind a noisy, messy, undomesticated animal
☐ I am prepared for a pet that gets around by flying
☐ I am ready for a challenging rather than an easy pet
☐ I understand the long lifespan and commitment necessary
☐ I am prepared for expensive upkeep costs
☐ I have researched different parrot species
☐ I have considered between bird store, breeder, or rescue
☐ I will make sure everything is great with one parrot before considering getting another
☐ I will consult an avian veterinarian for health topics
☐ I am ready for the thrill and challenge of investing into developing a well-behaved parrot!

Chapter 2: Situating the Parrot

Now that you have decided to acquire a parrot, and you know exactly what kind you want, you are ready to bring it home. This chapter is about the things you can do ahead of time and right when you bring the bird home to make the transition as smooth as possible.

If you purchased a baby parrot, most likely it does not come with its own cage and you had the opportunity to choose your own. It is best to bring the cage home before the parrot so that its new home is configured upon arrival. By setting the cage up ahead of time, not only is it easier to get the parrot situated but you may also realize that you are missing certain supplies and have another chance to get them. On the other hand, if you adopt a rehome/rescue parrot, most likely it comes with its own cage and there is no chance for setting things up before its arrival. Either way, this chapter is a guide on how to set things up so you can be sure things have been configured properly by the arrival of your new parrot.

The first thing you will need to decide is a location for the parrot's cage. This is a very important decision that will impact your parrot on a daily basis. Do you want the parrot to be in plain sight or in its own room? Should the cage be placed atop furniture or be free standing? How will the location affect the parrot? Is this an easy place to access for cleaning? These are all questions to consider when choosing a location. But, you also have to consider other factors for the parrot's safety such as having a secure location away from drafts and quiet at night so it can sleep.

Keep in mind when choosing a location that parrots require 12-14 hours of sleep at night and will most likely be asleep during some of the time you are still awake. For this reason, living rooms and other active places are not advisable.

Instead, choose a quiet out of the way place for the parrot's cage and a busier space for the parrot's play stand.

It is usually a good idea to put the bird's cage with at least one end facing a wall so that the parrot can have a sense of complete security from that direction. Windows are not a good place to be setting a parrot cage beside. Outside activity can frighten the parrot and lead to stress. The kitchen is definitely one place the parrot does not belong in due to fumes and other hazards. So with all these considerations in mind, choose a comfortable place where the parrot can reside.

Cages

Once you have chosen an approximate location, it is time to consider the cage itself. It is important to purchase a suitably sized cage for the parrot species you are bringing home. An excessively small cage can lead to behavioral issues. An excessively cheap cage can have poor features or quality.

Instead, follow the rule of thumb which is to purchase the largest cage you can afford with the correct bar spacing. Some people make the mistake of getting carried away and buying too big of a cage where the bar spacing is so wide that the parrot is at risk of getting its head stuck between the bars.

Parrot Cage Bar Spacing Chart

Species	Bar Spacing
Budgie, Lovebird, Parrotlet, Cockatiel	1/2"
Conures, Senegal, Caique, Ringneck, Quaker, Galah, Hahns	5/8"
Pionus, African Grey, Amazons, Eclectus, Smaller Cockatoos	3/4"
Macaws and Large Cockatoos	1" – 1-1/2"

So find the appropriate bar spacing for your size of parrot and find the largest cage you can afford above the minimum recommended size.

Remember that these cages typically last for dozens of years, or even the parrot's lifespan, so don't be stingy now or you will regret it later. Purchasing a cheaper cage now and replacing it with a better one later is much more expensive than just buying the right cage up front. Not only is it important to consider the size of the cage but also the shape, durability, material, ease of cleaning, and size of door. Some cages may be very good-looking and match your decor, but the door is small and it is difficult to clean. In the long run, you will regret an inconvenient cage far more than a less appealing looking one.

Separate food bowl doors are a good feature to look for. Even if you are comfortable with your bird, some day you may need someone else to take care of food and water who may not be. A grate at the bottom of the cage also serves this purpose and prevents the bird from gaining access to discarded food.

Keep in mind that the biggest purpose of a large cage is to be able to fill it up with perches and supplies. A large barren cage is hardly better than a small one. The large cage only enhances your parrot's behavior and well-being when it is filled with lots of things to do.

Things You Need

In addition to a cage, there are many other items you will need to purchase at the same time as the parrot or better yet in advance. Here is a quick summary of some things to consider: food supply (not only pellets, but also treats and alternative foods), perches, toys, first aid supplies (corn starch to stop bleeding), travel carrier, training perch, play stand (for out of cage time), cleaning supplies (make sure they are parrot safe and not toxic), and species specific books.

Discover stores that carry parrot supplies in your area and online. Knowing where to go to get it if you forget to buy something you need is important.

Finally, make sure you make contact with a local avian vet. Keep in mind that the majority of veterinarians are not experienced or certified to work with birds. Finding a qualified vet ahead of time is important should any sort of emergency arise.

Toys & Perches

When shopping for your upcoming parrot, you will need to purchase toys and perches to fill the cage. Since you are not aware of your new parrot's preferences (and neither is the parrot if it is a baby, because it has not experienced many of these things), it is best to provide as much variety as possible. Don't get carried away buying a lifetime supply; instead, focus on variety. Buy natural wooden perches with and without bark, NU Perches®, rope swings, bolt on ropes, and a grooming perch.

Diversify the toy selection by focusing on different materials and purposes. Provide a mixture of manufactured parrots toys such as wooden toys, plastic toys, natural toys, play toys, chew toys, and foraging toys. As you live with your new parrot, you will learn its preferences and be able to purchase more specific toys later on.

At first, it is better to provide excessively easy to destroy toys rather than tough ones. Most likely, the parrot is unfamiliar with toys and needs to learn on easy ones. Don't look for durability in toys because it is the destructive process that is the method of play for most parrots. Once the parrot learns to break easy toys, then you can attempt to provide more challenge with bigger/tougher toys.

With time, though, you will want to provide a greater variety of toys and perches. Get in the habit of entirely rearranging your parrot's cage every few months so that it does not become too dependent on any specific placement. At some point, the things you have may need replacement or become discontinued. The best way to prepare your parrot for inevitable changes is to regularly expose it to changes throughout its life.

Most parrots should have 5-8 perches and 8-12 toys in the cage at a time. Many behavioral issues can begin to be addressed with toys. It is important for a parrot to learn to be independent and preoccupied when in the cage to avoid screaming or feather mutilation issues. An abundance of perches exercises the feet and gives the parrot access to all those toys. Chapter 10 describes in greater detail how to use bird toys to improve behavior.

Hazards

Whether or not you set up the parrot's cage ahead of time, bird proofing your home must be done beforehand. We cannot accomplish good behavior from a parrot that is harmed by a household hazard. There are some hazards to parrots that are invisible yet deadly. These hazards must be dealt with preemptively and not as you go. Threats to your parrot's safety come in several forms: environmental, self-induced, and human. It is your responsibility to reduce as many of these threats as possible for the well-being of your pet.

Believe it or not, the greatest hazard to your parrot comes directly from humans in the household. Whether it's leaving the bathroom door open, cooking with the parrot out, forgetting to shut the cage, handling the parrot too roughly, etc., these dangers can easily be avoided with awareness and a little forethought. You have to think of parrot safety like having a clumsy toddler around, not just on the floor but in three dimensions. Don't for a second think that if the parrot is clipped these dangers do not apply. More often than not, it is clipped parrots that get hurt by elevated hazards than flighted ones.

Everyone in your household must get in the habit of closing doors, windows, bathrooms, and making sure the parrot is not out while cooking or during other hazardous activities. The biggest human factor is negligence or complacency which unfortunately is seen all too often. It is important not to get too comfortable and lower your guard because this is when something bad ends up happening.

There are some hazards that are so severe and uncontrollable, that not acquiring a parrot all together may be the only adequate defensive measure. If you have an open household with other pets that could harm parrots (cats, dogs, ferrets, snakes, and other predatory pets) that cannot be directly separated from the parrot at all times, you cannot safely introduce a parrot into this household. Even if these pets do not intentionally attempt to attack the parrot, it is just far too risky that their instincts and reflexes may cloud their "judgment" and lead to harming the parrot. Also, parrots cannot live in the household of a smoker; their respiratory systems are far too delicate.

Otherwise, most environmental factors can be resolved. There may be a cost of time, money, or patience to solve them. However, it is critical for the well-being of the parrot that these be taken care of preemptively and maintained for the span of its inhabitance. These include but are not limited to: all Teflon/PTFE based heating products (including pans, cookers, and hair products), self cleaning ovens, toxic plants, ceiling fans, and scented products. The simple solution is not to use candles, disable ceiling fans, check for and discard of toxic plants, avoid the self-cleaning feature on ovens, and discard Teflon/PTFE products while replacing them with "PTFE free" alternatives. Be careful when choosing new pans and cookware. Many pans will try to appear health conscious by saying they are PFOA free, lead free, and free of a whole list of other toxins but will fail to mention that they are PTFE free. This is a tricky way to divert attention from the fact that the pan actually does have the PTFE which is hazardous to parrots! Make sure you see the phrase "PTFE free" when choosing cookware and appliances that are safe to use in households with parrots.

Hide medications as parrots can chew through pill bottles. Avoid leaving food out and especially avoid leaving dangerous objects out as parrots are curious and can fly over to reach them. Take care not to have unscreened open windows. Never feed avocado, chocolate, coffee, or alcohol to parrots.

If these sorts of compromises seem excessive – which is perfectly understandable – you should reconsider parrot ownership because honestly this is one of the smaller challenges. There are far greater challenges ahead to test your dedication and this is just the beginning.

Bringing the Parrot Home

Now that you have taken all precautions for your parrot's safety and set up the parrot's cage, you are finally ready to bring the parrot home. Be sure to have your own carrier ready if the parrot does not come with one. Line the bottom of the carrier with paper towels.

If the expected travel time will exceed 3 hours, sprinkle bird food (the food that it is already accustomed to) on the bottom of the carrier. Also bring a cup or a bowl and a bottle of water. Do not drink from the same bottle that you will be using for the bird to prevent contamination with germs. Don't put water in the travel carrier or it will most likely spill. Instead, offer it from the cup every few hours. Another useful strategy is to put grapes or other watery fruits in the carrier bottom as sources of water.

Bring a towel with you and cover 3 out of 4 sides of the travel carrier. This way the bird can stay warm and feel protected while being able to look out. Secure the carrier in your car on the floor or on a seat with a seatbelt. Don't pay too much attention to the bird. Instead, focus on the road and getting home without wasting much time. As tempting as it might be, this is not the time to interact with the bird.

Once home, you will need to transfer the parrot from the travel carrier to the cage. Luckily, if you set the cage up ahead of time, the parrot can immediately be transferred rather than wait for hours while you try to assemble it and then realize something is missing, etc.

The actual transfer of parrot from carrier to cage can happen in several ways. If you know for a fact that the parrot is people-friendly, you can open the door and ask it to step up. Without training, this often is not the case or you may just not be certain if the parrot will come to you. So instead, you must swiftly make the transition.

Don't expect to be able to put the carrier door up to the cage and have the parrot just walk out and into the cage. The bird is most likely scared and will hunker down sooner than come out. Luring with food usually won't work in this circumstance. This is why the most likely course of action will require you to grab the bird and put it in the cage yourself. Open the carrier door partly and sneak your hand in to corner the bird and grab it from the back by the neck or shoulders (refer to photo on page 291). If you are uncomfortable using your bare hand, sneak a towel in through the open door or top of the carrier and drape it around the bird to take it out. Whatever you do, don't let the parrot get out of the carrier by itself, because then it will start flying or running around and you will have a much harder time catching the bird while the experience will be more prolonged and traumatic for the bird.

If somehow the parrot did slip out in the transfer process, you need to get hold of it promptly before this turns into a prolonged chase. First, try to have the bird step up onto your hand or a perch. Some birds may act scared and not step up when you ask, but the same bird may be willing to step up for a human if it ends up on the floor. If slowly coming up to the bird and asking it to step up on your hand fails, get a big towel or bed sheet. Dimming the lights may also help keep the bird from being able to get away. Toss the towel over the area where the bird is thus entrapping it. Then use your hands to scoop the towel together and get a hold of the bird. Transfer the parrot to the cage. Give the parrot a break for several hours before any further interaction. It is important to keep the trauma of this initial experience to a minimum but don't worry about it too much. We will rectify all of this and make amends in coming chapters. The unpleasant experience of the first carrier to cage transfer is unavoidable, so the best you can do is make it swift and relatively painless. Most likely, in the mayhem of the entire homecoming, the fact that you grabbed the bird will not be remembered as much amidst the entire situation.

Chapter 2 Checklist:

- ☐ Get your parrot supplies ahead of time
- ☐ Choose a good/quiet location for the cage
- ☐ Get the biggest cage you can get
- ☐ Ensure the cage bar spacing is suitable for your species
- ☐ Get and hang a variety of toys/perches in the cage
- ☐ 5-8 perches of various types
- ☐ 8-12 parrot toys
- ☐ Eliminate household hazards
- ☐ Keep cats, dogs, or other pets away from the parrot
- ☐ No smoking
- ☐ No Teflon/PTFE cookware or appliances
- ☐ Hide hazardous foods, objects, and medications
- ☐ Transfer parrot from carrier to cage swiftly
- ☐ Give the parrot a chance to settle down

Chapter 3: Early Interactions

First impressions play a big role in establishing the relationship that you will have with your parrot. Bad experiences can be amended but oftentimes that is significantly more difficult than doing things right in the first place.

There is usually a lot of excitement at the arrival of a new pet but it is important to maintain control over this and not allow it to become overwhelming for the bird. Keep in mind that parrots coming from stores usually have never been in a home. Parrots coming from breeders may be used to one home but have never been in another. Parrots being rehomed from other owners or rescues may have had a troubling past or just as well a good past, but now their entire lifestyle is being jumbled around. Thus it is very important not to expect or assume that the bird is a ready-to-go pet. Instead, just assume that it is scared and needs to develop trust.

Please realize that in the first hours, days, and weeks, the new parrot's history with you is very brief. For this reason, all existing experiences dominate a large percent of the interactions that the parrot has had in its new environment. Therefore, avoiding bad experiences must be a top priority. Simply put, do your best to avoid scaring the parrot and take care that others don't either. It is better to err on the side of excess caution than to create a bad first impression that will take a lot more effort to amend.

Since the parrot is still learning about you – and, if it is young, humans in general – it is important to be very open about your intentions. Although the parrot does not understand things that you are saying, it may gain some comfort in the tone of your voice. Talking to the bird about what you are going to do can't hurt. Make your movements slow and predictable. Always try to start your approach from as far away as possible and at a slow pace. In the early days, whenever you or anyone in your household needs to walk past the parrot's cage, try to do it slowly. Pass by the cage from as far away as possible. Avoid looking at the bird as tempting as that might be. Parrots can tell predators by their eyes. Predators tend to have binocular vision with two forward facing eyes and human eyes are set the same way. Because of this, until a parrot is accustomed to humans, this type of gaze may cause the bird to feel vulnerable and that is the opposite of the comfort that we are trying to establish. The best strategy is to pretend the parrot does not exist when you are walking by the cage and this will give the parrot a chance to think that it is well hidden in the forest that is its cage.

When you approach your parrot's cage with the intention of looking, interacting, changing food/water, or handling the bird, make slow and deliberate steps starting from as far away as possible. Don't look straight at the bird as you approach. Instead, try to look away while taking occasional glances in its direction. If the parrot appears very scared, stop periodically before continuing closer. Signs to look for that demonstrate substantial levels of fear include shaking, cowering in a corner, frantic movement, and worst of all trying to fly in the cage while crashing into cage bars. A little bit of shaking, pacing, or cowering is tolerable but do not approach so closely or suddenly that the parrot crashes around in the cage. If signs of fear continue growing as you approach, stop for a while where you are and wait for the bird to calm down a little. Then slowly sneak your way closer with imperceptible baby steps.

Another approach that is very good is to sit in a chair in the bird's sight and read a book. A rolling chair is most suited for this exercise, but any chair will do. Start by setting up the chair far away, ignore the bird, and do your own thing. Every few minutes slide your chair a little bit closer toward the bird and go back to what you were doing. All this time, you are getting closer to the bird and yet showing no intent of doing anything to it, so trust should improve. You may need to repeat this process over the span of a few days until you can sit right by the parrot's cage and it will be OK with you doing so.

Once you can sit or stand by the parrot's cage without the bird showing major signs of fear, you can begin to interact with it more. You can talk to the parrot, watch it, and show toys/objects to the bird. An easy way to approach this is to take a handful of household objects and tell your bird what they are, what they are used for, etc. This will give you something to talk about and if the parrot happens to learn to say these things, it will be cute. For example, "Hey Polly, look at this. This is a book. I have a book. Books are made from paper and they have writing on them. Do you see my book? My book is blue." This way the bird learns your voice, becomes accustomed to your presence, learns that you are nonthreatening, and possibly even learns to say the word "book". Since parrots like to imitate the sounds around them, they happen to also be really good listeners. By giving your parrot something to listen to, as long as it isn't terribly scared to begin with, this may take its mind off your presence while it is busy listening. As you progress, slowly start holding your hand outside the cage and eventually get to a point where you can rest your hand on the bird's cage while you talk to it. Get the bird used to the presence of your hands to ensure success at later stages when the bird will interact with them.

It may be a matter of a few hours to weeks until you can put your hands on the parrot's cage without causing it to panic. Of course, the sooner this can be achieved the better, because inevitably you're going to have to touch the cage in order to change food & water daily. When you do come to change food/water and clean, use methods similar to the ones previously mentioned to go about the tasks while ignoring the bird. Unfortunately, you may have to push past the parrot's comfort boundaries by doing that. Two steps forward, one step back. That is how it's going to work until you have gained the bird's most basic level of trust.

Now if you're working with an already tame or baby bird, you may be able to breeze through the basic desensitization steps in a matter of minutes or hours and have the parrot out of the cage on the very first day. If this is the case, just be sure to avoid doing scary things rapidly. I caution you not to take the bird's tameness for granted and skip anything. It is better to err on the side of caution and push the parrot less than it is capable of than to make the mistake of scaring it by pushing too much.

Don't feel pressure or even a necessity to take the parrot out of the cage. It is more important to let the parrot settle down and develop hands-off trust than to get the bird out of the cage. Forcing the bird out of the cage will work against your taming progress. On the other hand, don't leave the cage door open for the parrot to venture out on its own either. The goal is to build trust until you are able to do a little training and take the bird in and out of the cage comfortably.

Nutrition & Diet

As the parrot is getting established in your home, this is also a good time to begin introducing the bird to an assortment of healthy foods. In the first days with you, just feed the bird whatever it was accustomed to eating from wherever it came. The first day or two, it may not eat at all, but as long as you see signs that the bird is eating by the third day, things are fine. Look for pellet crumbs, empty seed shells, missing food, and droppings at the cage bottom for signs that the bird is eating. Most likely the bird will be too shy to eat in your presence, so you will not get to see it eating for yourself.

Within a week of being with you and stable on its existing diet, it is time to begin offering different foods to the parrot. For now, continue providing the bird's staple food all day long, but in a different dish offer alternate foods for the parrot to try. A good place to start for new foods is fruits and vegetables. Remember that avocado, onions, tomatoes, and garlic should never be fed to a bird. Thoroughly wash fruits/vegetables and remove the skin if there is any. Cut some small bits and offer them to the parrot in a dish. Try offering broccoli, cauliflower, carrot, corn, snap peas, pepper, apple, banana, and grapes to start. There is no need to give this all at once. Try to introduce a different food once or twice a day by itself so that the parrot can really focus on it.

If the parrot is not readily trying new foods, you can try chopping them up really fine and rolling them around in seeds or pellets (whichever the parrot came to you eating). Besides fruits and vegetables, offer other plain human foods. Some things to try include pasta, rice, bread, crackers, oatmeal, sweet potato, and eggs. Don't serve foods with any seasoning, sauce, or spice. Chocolate is deadly and must not be served. Nor foods that contain it such as chocolate chip cookies. Finally, avoid highly sweet foods with refined sugar such as cookies, cake, candy, or drinks because they will make the parrot way too hyper. Hyper parrots are not well-behaved parrots, so sugary foods and sweetened pellets should be avoided. Don't give anything but water for your parrot to drink.

Now when it comes to optimal diet and parrot nutrition, I have to recommend that you consult an avian veterinarian and do research on your specific species. What may be a suitable diet for one parrot species may be too fatty for another. Briefly, I will just mention that for most parrots a pellet diet is a good basis with some supplemental foods. Parrots are really picky and will eat foods in their order of preference, often starting with the least healthy foods. Since the food is plentiful and replenished daily, the bird ends up getting away with eating all the "junk food" and avoiding healthy things. A pellet diet forces the parrot to get balanced nutrition in every bite without the ability to pick things apart and eat only what it likes.

Many people do not realize that having well-behaved parrots starts with what they eat. Having a healthy parrot is the basis of it all. Feeding the parrot rich foods is important but should be done in moderation. Having an overfed hyperactive parrot is no better than a malnourished lethargic one.

Budgies and cockatiels, however, require a predominantly seed-based diet. A seed diet for larger parrots is not healthy and counterproductive for training. Read up on the nutritional requirements of your species, consult other owners of similar parrots, or ask an avian veterinarian.

Treats

It is also important to establish treats for your parrot. You will at times want to allow your parrot to indulge, and treats will be a necessary element for creating motivation for the parrot to cooperate with you. The thing many people don't realize though is that the parrot may not even know what a treat is. So it is up to both the owner and the parrot to make this discovery together.

First I would like to caution you to stay away from manufactured "bird treats." Most of the time they are loaded with fat and sugar (which makes it no wonder that any bird would quickly take to them) and they are terribly unhealthy. There are plenty of other healthy treats your parrot will take just as readily. Many parrots already have a lot more energy than we can cope with, so when we are looking for good behavior from them, feeding them sugary foods is not the answer. Imagine the consequences of feeding a young child a box of donuts and candy. You can expect something similar with a parrot. But instead of just running around in 2D, a hyperactive parrot will be flying around a lot in 3D as well as making a lot more noise.

The exact items that your parrot likes will be somewhat specific to the individual, but here is a list of some foods to try so that you could learn what your parrot likes best. Budgies, cockatiels, other parakeets, and very small parrots love millet spray. You don't have to look much further because that is a very successful treat for those birds. For all larger parrots, you should test a mix of seeds, nuts, human foods, and fruit. An easy way to start is to buy a typical parrot seed mix to use exclusively for treats. Also, buy some walnuts, almonds, pistachios, other nuts, and dried fruit. Try offering nuts both in the shell and out. Avoid peanuts entirely, however. Many parrots enjoy the challenge of opening a nut themselves, but some parrots just never had the experience and don't realize that a surprise awaits them inside the shell until you show them. At first, offer these foods in the cage for a few days (separately or together) but in moderation. After a few days, mix all the treat foods you are testing in a bowl and offer to your parrot in the cage. Watch and remember the order in which the parrot eats the foods because this usually correlates to their order of preference. For example, if it eats the sunflower seeds first, then the cashews, then the safflower seeds, but leaves everything else, then that is its preference order. Keep this in mind, because you don't want to always give your parrot its most favorite treat. In general you should use secondary or other less favored treats, saving the favorite ones for special times.

If your parrot is big enough that it ought to be able to crack open nuts but doesn't want to, here is a way to teach the parrot to open nuts. Start with softer shelled nuts like almonds. Use a nut cracker to crack the nut open, but do this only partially. Offer the pre-cracked nut to the bird. The parrot will find a way to clear the nut out and learn what to do. With time you can provide less and less help. Offer more and more challenging nuts to keep the parrot engaged.

Now that you have established what foods are your parrot's favorites, the next step is never to provide them except for when your parrot is offering good behavior as will be later discussed in this book. Resist the temptation to give treats for no reason and make sure that other people don't do this either. Although many people enjoy the concept of "spoiling their pets," this ultimately will backfire and lead to the kind of parrot that would not be regarded by most as "well-behaved" though this is our ultimate goal.

Sleep

Don't underestimate the importance of adequate durations of uninterrupted sleep for companion parrots. They require 12-14 hours of sleep at night. This is a fair bit more than humans usually sleep. Birds have a supercharged body that runs at the equivalent of human fever temperatures and human running heartbeats while the bird is at rest. So, they need greater amounts of rest to make up for this high paced metabolism. Since most parrot species are endemic to equatorial regions, it is no wonder where the 12 hour figure comes from because that is the typical day/night span on the equator. So for these reasons, it is critical that parrots receive at least 12 hours of scheduled sleep every night.

The fact that parrots sleep for so long may be inconvenient to the owner and may make the parrot unavailable for play time when the owner is still awake, but it is something you must accept with this type of pet. We can't expect good behavior from a sleep deprived animal. An easy rule of thumb for considering the schedule for a parrot's sleep is to take the same hour and schedule sleep from the PM of that hour to the AM. For example if a parrot goes to sleep at 9PM, then it must not be wakened until 9AM.

If a separate dark room cannot be provided to the parrot for sleep, it will be necessary to cover the cage with a dark sheet to ensure that the parrot can receive an adequate amount of darkness for sleep. A breathable black king size sheet from a cheap store is a convenient choice for a cage cover. If possible, cover windows as well. Bright sunlight leaking through the windows, even with a cage cover, is likely to wake the parrot too early for it to receive adequate rest. The steadiness of scheduled sleep every night is as important as the duration.

Desensitization

Parrots are prey species so their fear and caution is not surprising. In the wild they need to be protective for survival. In the home, these instincts must be dealt with accordingly. How you alleviate this stress will play a pivotal role in your relationship with your pet.

Rather than scaring a parrot with exposure to something novel all at once, the process of desensitization breaks a potentially frightening experience down into smaller less terrifying doses until the parrot is no longer scared. Here is why it is important to follow this process and not allow a parrot to get too scared. Let's say a parrot is scared of boxes and someone walks in with a box and comes toward the parrot. As the growing level of fear increases, the parrot becomes frantic and starts crashing into the bars of the cage. Even though the parrot ended up doing this to itself (which in the wild would be the natural response of simply flying away from anything it fears), the parrot will develop a greater fear of that box or possibly even the human wielding it. Next time a box is brought out, the parrot relives the terror and pain it went through last time it encountered one and the process starts all over again. These types of patterns become difficult to break as any additional exposure to the object the parrot fears immediately elicits an overwhelming response that turns into a self-fulfilling prophecy. One terrifying experience can thus develop a phobia, which can take months or years to reverse. So it is critical to avoid ever exposing your parrot to excessively terrifying experiences.

Desensitization, on the other hand breaks the fear down into manageable stages, preventing a state of panic that will carry over to future encounters. The result of desensitization should always be a less fearful reaction in subsequent encounters. As you become more experienced and more familiar with your individual parrot, gauging fear levels should become easier. If you are not familiar with the subtle signs, it is safest to assume your parrot is fearful and work at a comfortably slow pace rather than overdoing it. Remember that a parrot will go through many milder levels of fear before it is throwing itself at the cage bars, so don't automatically assume that the absence of frantic behavior means the parrot is not experiencing any fear.

Ultimately the goal of all this desensitization is to be able to gain your parrot's trust to the extent that it will take treats from your hand through the cage bars. Once the parrot begins seeing you not only as nonthreatening but also as a source of good things, your relationship will improve much more rapidly. Since you've been establishing what treats your parrot enjoys in parallel to the desensitization process, by the time you can touch your parrot's cage, you'll also know what to offer.

Note that everything recommended until this point is conducted with the parrot inside the cage. Except for the hideous but necessary grabbing in order to get the bird into the cage for the first time, no further rough handling is ever induced. There is no point in getting or forcing the parrot out of the cage until it is desensitized to the point that it is calm in your presence. Letting a frantic parrot out of the cage simply to flee from you by flying, running, hiding, or biting accomplishes nothing. Worse yet, it increases the number of bad experiences that the bird has with you and makes the pattern more difficult to overcome. Likewise, don't let the parrot come out of its cage by itself, because, until you begin a training program, you're not going to have a reasonable way to get the parrot back into the cage. Don't forget that if you acquired an already tame bird (namely from a breeder, store, or reliable home), then these desensitization steps may be achieved in as little as a few hours or days and then you're on your way.

When you have reached the point that you can come up to your parrot's cage, touch the cage, change the food, and possibly even touch the parrot through the bars or at least offer treats, you are ready to move onward to basic training. If, however, you are not able to come close to the bird without it becoming terribly uneasy, then give it some more time. Have patience because these early desensitization stages are the hardest and take the longest amount of time. Once you alleviate the major fear that your parrot has, everything will move much more quickly.

Baby Parrots

If you get your parrot as a baby from a store or breeder, here are a few more suggestions to use early on. The remainder of the advice in this book will be just as relevant once the bird matures.

The baby stage for a parrot will vary by species. Smaller parrots will generally move out of it by around 6 months old. Medium parrots such as Amazons and Greys: closer to a year old. Large parrots such as Macaws may continue exhibiting baby behavior well into 2 years old.

During the baby stage, parrots learn a bit differently. At this age, the parrot does not normally have to do much in order to be fed. Mama bird comes over and stuffs food into the baby's mouth. It takes some time for the bird to transition to thinking on its own and feeding itself. During this baby stage, the parrot soaks in knowledge like a sponge. However, it does not necessarily act on the information. Training is often ineffective at this age because the bird does not yet have enough self-interest to try to earn its own treats.

When you have an already friendly baby from a store or breeder, consider yourself lucky. Enjoy the baby phase and the interaction you can achieve. However, <u>do not</u> take this behavior for granted. Once the baby age wears off, this bird will mature into a wild adult parrot no matter what. The baby that would never bite, may bite you. The baby that always liked coming out of the cage, may hunker down. Following the methodology recommended in this book before the baby becomes a full adult is the best way of ensuring that the friendly behavior you started with can stick for the long run.

On the other hand, sometimes you get a baby bird that isn't so friendly. Yet, the bird is too young to be taught through training because it does not have enough motivation at this age. What a dilemma. The bird doesn't allow handling and is not mature enough for training. The number one best solution in this case is patience. Give the bird a little time to mature and the training will work much better. Now this does not mean that you should not begin training from early on. However, the training will not be anywhere near as effective and quick as it will be with a bird that is past the baby age. What will happen is that the training will be so slow that the bird will grow up by the time you are close to success and then the training will really start to work effectively.

In either case, whether a baby bird is friendly or not, you should primarily focus on exploring things with your bird. You will always have time to do training, build a relationship, and develop a well-behaved parrot. Don't try to force this early on before the bird is ready for it. Instead, use this age when the bird is ready to explore as an opportunity and as an exciting part of bird ownership.

You will want to explore foods, toys, people, places, and objects to the maximum extent. Get your parrot to sample as many different foods as possible. Right now, it is less important to feed the best food than to feed as many different varieties of foods. The goal is to develop a healthy desire to eat various foods so that the parrot does not become too choosy later on. Preferences usually stick. Developing a preference for variety will allow you to modify and optimize the diet over time. Try feeding several different brands of pellets. Offer a variety of seeds, nuts, and fruits in moderation. Encourage eating vegetables and other healthy foods. Be a part of the experience. Show the parrot how much you enjoy each food you offer by eating some yourself. At this age, the parrot is looking to those around it for advice on how to be.

In addition to food, this is a great time to help the parrot explore a variety of perches and toys. With the parrot in the cage, hold bird toys in your hand. You can show different parts and talk to the parrot about the toy. For example, "wow, look at this amazing toy. It has wood, paper, plastic, and string. This piece of wood is red and this piece is blue. I like breaking wood." Break the toy in your hands yourself. Show the parrot how it is done. This is much better encouragement for the bird to learn to play with bird toys than watching you handle your keyboard, phone, or remote. The parrot will learn the wrong things to play with if it does not see you "play" with the things that birds should ideally grow up playing with instead.

Finally, try to have many different faces around. This does not mean other people should necessarily touch or handle the parrot. If the parrot is uncomfortable, it is not worth forcing interaction with people. However, just becoming familiar with the fact that there are other people in the world and they aren't mean is already an important introduction. If you are able to take the parrot outside in a travel cage for walks and car rides, that is a further opportunity to help the parrot experience more of the world while growing up.

It won't be long until the parrot is old enough that training can be more effective and you will be right on track with the more formal education in good pet behavior.

Chapter 3 Checklist:

- ☐ Make a good first impression by avoiding making a bad one
- ☐ Transfer the bird into the cage promptly the first time
- ☐ Approach the cage slowly
- ☐ Avoid direct eye contact at first
- ☐ Approach the bird gradually in a rolling chair
- ☐ Offer a variety of foods for your bird to try
- ☐ Discover the birds' favorite treats after a few days
- ☐ Save treats exclusively for good behavior and training
- ☐ 12 hours of sleep every day, year round
- ☐ Desensitize parrots to new objects slowly
- ☐ Explore foods, toys, perches, people, places, and objects with baby parrots and save training for later

Chapter 4: Taming & Training

Parrot training is useful and fun both for people and the pet parrot! It is a way of teaching appropriate behavior in the home while also improving communication, providing enrichment, and giving purpose.

While the end goal might be to have a relationship with a well-behaved parrot, training will help get you there. It will teach the parrot the way to live harmoniously in the human home. But, more importantly, training will create the trust necessary to develop your own personal relationship.

You see, parrots are not domesticated. Further still, they are prey animals. The lack of domestication makes them lack any innate loyalty toward humans. The fact that they are prey animals, makes them skittish and untrusting. It takes a long time to build trust, but only a short time to lose it. This makes parrots so much different than a cat, dog, or even hamster.

Parrots tend to be very social, which is not only redeeming, but also an exciting part of their character. They usually like to see what is going on and even respond with vocalizations or dances. However, don't let that fool you. Just because a parrot likes someone and engages remotely, does not mean that the parrot is okay with physical contact.

Quite often, people mistakenly misinterpret a parrot's excited interaction with them as an invitation to touch or pick up the bird. After reaching in to touch, a painful bite ensues!

Other times, a parrot wants nothing to do with people. It could be an older parrot, from a rescue, a rehomed parrot from a previous owner, or even a parrot you've had a long time and just grew disconnected with over time.

It could even be an easy-going baby parrot that lets you do anything. This baby parrot will still mature into a wild, undomesticated, adult parrot with a mind of its own.

Regardless of the parrot's history or current behavior, training will be beneficial to you and your parrot. It can bring more structure, communication, understanding, and reliability to both you and the bird. Practicing the behavior you would like your parrot to exhibit through training helps the parrot learn to behave as such throughout the day. Practice makes perfect.

There are two sides to working on behavior: taming and training. Training is the process of teaching a specific behavior such as stepping onto your hand. Taming, on the other hand, is the process of reducing or eliminating existing behavior such as fleeing or biting. You will need to use both in order to have the parrot learn to behave in ways more suitable for the home and less in ways suitable for the wild.

The training process appeals to a parrot's intellect and innate problem solving capacity. Parrots need an outlet for both their physical and mental energy. Not only will you get to exercise the parrot's brain, you will also be teaching better behavior for the long run.

Training Setup

The process of parrot training is in itself challenging and time consuming. Whenever it is possible to improve training effectiveness through things other than spending time/effort doing more training, it is worth it. This is where having a good training setup can spare you extra effort.

Start with eliminating as many distractions as possible. Every item to look at and sound to listen to is competing with your training effort. Minimizing the distractions will maximize your training success.

Until you are able to take your parrot out of the cage, you will be faced with training in a distracting environment. However, once you are able to move the bird, training should go smoother in a dedicated training area.

To set up a training area, choose the least distracting place in your home you can find. This might be a guest room, a hallway, or even a bathroom. Find a room with few windows or windows that are covered to avoid the parrot getting preoccupied with what is going on outside. Choose a room where you can be alone with the parrot. It is not easy to train a parrot if someone next to you is on the phone, watching TV, cooking, or talking to you. Choose the quietest and emptiest place for your training sessions.

Initially, you may need to train the parrot inside the cage before you are ready to have the bird out. If the location where the cage is normally is too hectic, you may need to move the cage to a more suitable training area. Give the bird time to get used to the new location before starting training.

Once you are able to take the parrot out of the cage, the first distraction to eliminate is the cage itself. Parrots can have a strong territorial relationship with their cage. They might want to go back inside or bite intruders that come near. For these reasons, it is best to train away from the cage and with the cage out of sight.

Avoid training on tree stands and other "bird furniture" that is not meant for training (more about this in Chapter 10). Do not train the parrot on any human furniture you would not want the parrot to go on all the time. Training on a table, except for some specific tricks that involve training on a surface, is not advised.

The best place for training a parrot is on a dedicated Parrot Wizard Parrot Training Perch. These bird stands are distraction free and height adjustable. There are no toys or distractions. It is just a perch freestanding in the air. The perch is short, so the parrot does not have anywhere to venture off to. This removes other activities from the parrot's immediate vicinity and makes it more likely the parrot will pay attention during the training.

The adjustable height of Training Perches™ allows you to set the parrot at the most comfortable height for you. Having the parrot too low makes it uncomfortable for you to reach. Setting the parrot too high is the same problem plus the risk of possibly getting bit in the face. The optimal height to set a parrot during training is with the parrot's head just below your chin (photo on page 292). From this height, you will have a good view of the parrot and easy reach with your hands. The height of the perch will depend on the size of the parrot. Larger parrots need to be set lower to keep the head at the same height as a smaller parrot.

An alternative for a Training Perch™ can be a tabletop perch, a chair back, or a freestanding perch. Avoid training on the cage, floor, furniture, or on your hand. Whether you use a purpose-built Training Perch™ or a makeshift one, keep your perch exclusive to the purpose of training. Do not use it for the bird to just sit or hang out on. This will help ensure that the bird will get into the mood to train and learn whenever brought to the training perch.

The more dedicated and comfortable your training perch and training setup are, the more ready for successful training you and your parrot will be.

Training Schedule

Like a good training setup, a training schedule will also improve focus and learning. Things start out slow as you do not have a routine to go on. But, as the training schedule becomes routine, the parrot will be more eager to partake in the training following the predictable schedule.

Start by establishing a training schedule. There will be times of the day when the parrot is more responsive to training than others. It will vary with every bird, but in general morning and evening are good training times. Middle of the day and at night are not.

Do your training prior to feedings because this is when the parrot will be the most eager to earn treats. You can train your parrot one or two times a day. If you do more than that, the bird may burn out and actually train less effectively. Establish a consistency in your training schedule so that the parrot knows to expect it and is ready to train.

If possible, try to train every day. 5-6 days a week of daily training helps build a good routine. However, take one or two days a week off from training so that both you and the parrot can recharge. An occasional rest from training can aid in the process and also keep the parrot from growing too used to a set routine.

Keep training sessions short, especially in the beginning. New birds and young birds tend to have short attention spans. This will be exercised and extended through practice. But initially, the sessions can be quite short. The first training sessions are as much about building stamina for longer training as for teaching a particular skill.

Your first training session may only last a minute. Subsequent sessions might last 2, 4, and 5 minutes which is already big progress. 10 minutes of training is a good duration to build up to for the long run. 30 minutes of training is reserved for a seasoned parrot. More than that is both unnecessary and ineffective.

Ultimately, the parrot will set the duration of the training session with its responsiveness. While the parrot is focused and the training is effective, you can keep going. However, you should try to end the training while the parrot is doing well and not after the success is diminishing. It may be hard to predict when this will happen, so best to err on terminating the training session a bit early rather than late. You do not want the parrot to discover that cooperating during training is unimportant. If your training sessions go on for too long and you are begging the parrot to keep paying attention, the parrot will discover that it will still be rewarded even without trying. So, quit while you're ahead. Your next training will be better for it.

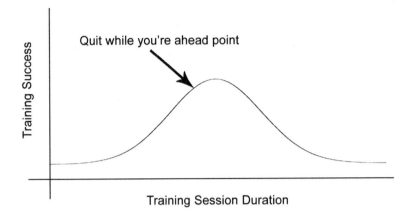

Positive Reinforcement

The most effective operant method of training parrots is through the use of positive reinforcement. This helps get the parrot to learn to cooperate voluntarily and build good habits. It also avoids stressing the parrot out or causing behavioral repercussions.

Positive reinforcement means to give or do something that increases behavior. The simplest example of positive reinforcement is to give a parrot a treat every time it steps up so the parrot becomes more likely to step up in the future.

The concept of positive reinforcement is result driven. If giving or doing something in response to a behavior does not increase it, then it was not actually positive reinforcement. If you give a parrot kisses whenever it steps up and the parrot is no more likely to step up voluntarily, then kisses may not be acting as positive reinforcement.

Negative reinforcement means to stop doing something or take something away so that behavior increases. Largely, this method should be avoided because we want to avoid the parrot being in a state of discomfort in the first place.

Punishment

Punishment involves the reduction of behavior. This is the opposite of reinforcement which increases behavior. Positive punishment is to give or do something that decreases behavior. Negative punishment is to stop doing something or take something away that decreases behavior. The most important thing to learn about punishment with parrots is to avoid it both deliberately and inadvertently. Because parrots are prey animals, most acts of punishment will confirm the parrot's innate fears of humans and diminish trust. Worse yet, many attempts of punishment may only exacerbate the problem. For example, pushing a parrot with a stick in response to biting is actually more likely to make the parrot bite because it feels the need to defend itself.

Unlike punishment, which is a learning process that reduces behavior, acts of punishment are when the person tries to respond in a way that they think would reduce unwanted behavior but does not. Acts of punishment generally have to do with retaliation and having a feeling of control. However, what is the point of taking frustration out on a confused little animal? If the bird does not reduce behavior as a response, it will only cause more acts of punishment, strain the relationship, and make good parrot behavior even more remote.

There are many unintended consequences of using any form of punishment on parrots. Spraying a parrot with water as punishment is likely to make a parrot fearful of water and then you would not be able to give the parrot a friendly shower. Sticking the parrot in the cage as punishment for misbehaving may make the parrot uncomfortable with the cage and hate being put away. "Random biting" is largely driven by prior acts of punishment, even inadvertent.

Since parrots are not domesticated, they do not see acts of punishment as a consequence for their behavior. Instead, it only makes them even more uncomfortable around humans. An uncomfortable parrot will only become a more misbehaved parrot.

If you want to work toward having a trusting well-behaved parrot, you have to avoid punishment. Instead of being the nagging parent who says "no, no, no" to everything the parrot does, be the cool friend who provides encouragement and says "yes"! This does not mean to give the parrot the run of the house. It just means to set up the environment, training, and lifestyle such that the things that the parrot is encouraged to do are more in line with pet life in the home.

Prevention

The most effective method for not having unwanted parrot behavior is prevention. Prevent the parrot from engaging in the unwanted behavior in the first place. When the parrot is prevented from trying the unwanted behavior or engaging in it, the parrot is prevented from developing a preference for engaging in that unwanted behavior in the future. Preventing unwanted behavior prevents the temptation to revert to acts of punishment that will hurt your relationship and likely not even reduce the unwanted behavior.

Get used to thinking in terms of prevention. If you do not want your parrot to chew your phone, don't leave your phone out. If you do not want your parrot chewing on the moldings, give your parrot even easier to chew wooden toys on a tree stand. If you do not want a parrot to scream, provide quiet activities to partake in such as talking, foraging, or training. Prevention is the genuine method for avoiding both natural and learned undesirable behavior from pet parrots. It is the best way to avoid the parrot doing things you would consider to be bad and to help the parrot learn how to behave instead. More about effective use of prevention in Chapters 8 and 10.

Motivation

In order for a reward to be reinforcing, the parrot has to actually want it. If you give a parrot something that you think it wants but in reality it doesn't, this won't lead to positive reinforcement and therefore the parrot will not learn to do what you want. Likewise, if you give something that the parrot might want but already has in abundance, it won't work. For example if a parrot is fed pellets all day, just ate, and now you offer a pellet as a reward for training, it will be meaningless and the parrot won't learn. If you normally feed treat foods to the parrot in the cage, then these won't be useful for training either.

You must only give your parrot treats and things reserved for use as rewards in response to desirable behavior.

Desirable behavior can be anything from performing a trick to going back into the cage. Desirable behavior can even be doing nothing undesirable at the moment. For example, sitting quietly in the cage is desirable while throwing a screaming fit is not. You want to try to make sure that the parrot receives as many rewards and things it wants from you rather than out of nowhere. This will give you many more opportunities to encourage and drive good behavior.

At every training session, check that the parrot wants the treat you expect to be using. Offer the treat from the side at some distance and see if the parrot will walk over to take it. If not, try a different treat in case the parrot prefers something else this time. If the parrot is not interested in various treats, this may not be the right time to do the training. Try at a different time. If the parrot never wants treats, put greater emphasis on ensuring you have a healthy feeding schedule in place.

The positive reinforcement training approach does not deprive a parrot of anything but just shifts the time when the parrot receives things. In the training approach, the parrot receives goodies (the sum of all desired things such as treats, toys, attention, etc.) in the vicinity of good behavior. If the parrot wants a seed, it will be able to politely ask for it by performing a trick or talking. Thus the human gets a well-behaved parrot and the parrot still gets to have the goodies we'd otherwise like to provide.

Although toys, scratches, attention, and other things could be used as rewards in training, favorite food is by far the easiest to use for multiple reasons. First of all, a parrot's necessity to eat predictably reoccurs daily. It is the easiest and often the most effective reinforcer. It can be applied by different people (even people the parrot doesn't know or like) and is the most effective reward universally for all readers. Furthermore, food can be accurately and predictably regulated while desire for other reinforcers is much more limited. For these reasons I urge you to use the bird's favorite food as your primary reward for training, but if you discover effectiveness in other forms, use them to maintain behavior after it is learned.

The most common problem I hear from parrot owners attempting to use food as a motivator is that the parrot doesn't want it. The parrot either doesn't take the food or drops it without eating it. Either way, this won't teach the parrot anything because it is not reinforcing. The reason is quite simple and obvious but not obvious enough to many: the parrot is overfed.

Healthy Feeding

Healthy feeding is a key ingredient to success in parrot training, overall parrot health, reducing some unwanted behavior, and for cultivating the well-behaved parrot. Healthy feeding is not just what you feed, but also how you feed it, when, and how much! (photo on page 291)

I can only offer a broad introduction on the topic of what to feed parrots. There are many feeding options available and they will vary with location, budget, size/species of bird.

For budgies and cockatiels, a largely seed diet is typical and adequate. Otherwise, most parrot species do well on a largely pelleted diet. While there are some subtle differences between pellet brands, the difference between the best and worst pelleted diet is subtle compared to the difference between a seed and a pellet diet. Except for budgies and cockatiels, seeds should be saved entirely for use as treat foods. Nuts, dried fruit, pasta, and most human foods should also be saved only for treats.

Fresh foods add enrichment, flavor, and diversity to your parrot's diet. A variety of vegetables, leafy greens, and some fruits are good for all parrots in moderation. Broccoli, carrots, kale, spinach, sweet pepper, and squash are very nutritious and a great place to start. Flax seed, hemp seed, cooked quinoa, and whole grains are another great addition to some of the fresh foods you offer to your parrot. Those can be soaked or sprouted to enhance nutrition.

Keep in mind that some species such as eclectus and lories require specialized diets. For all parrots, consult with an avian veterinarian for feedback on your parrot's nutrition based on measurements from blood work results and condition.

Keeping track of your parrot's weight is a great way to get feedback on feeding and health. Unexpected weight loss could be an early-warning sign of illness. It is best to get a scale with a perch to make weighing your parrot a breeze.

When to feed parrots is one of the more overlooked aspects of healthy feeding. Filling a few food bowls and leaving them in the cage all day long is neither good for behavior nor for health. In the wild, parrots typically feed twice a day: in the morning and in the evening. They are not meant to be eating all day long. However, out of boredom and availability, overeating and obesity are common problems in captivity. For these reasons, it is best that you feed your parrot scheduled meals twice a day. One in the morning and one in the evening.

Food should be available all day long for baby, sick, or injured parrots. As the baby parrot starts to mature, you can transition to scheduled feedings by going to three meals a day and then two. The same can apply for the first few weeks of bringing any new parrot home.

There is no reason to leave food in the cage at night (unless you know the night ahead that you won't be able to feed the bird in the morning). Food left in the cage overnight is only spoiling or attracting bugs. Do not leave any food in the parrot's cage at night.

By morning, the parrot will awaken from a night long fast and be ready to eat. This is an opportunity to perform some effective training with treats and/or have the parrot out of the cage for a bit. However, other than treats for behavior, do not feed the parrot out of the cage. When you are about ready to put the parrot away and leave to go to school or work, this is the time to feed the bird. The parrot will have a good incentive to go back into the cage to receive the first meal, and this will quickly turn into a normal routine.

Feed the parrot a healthy staple diet in a bowl in the cage for 15-30 minutes. Either when the parrot is finished eating or the time has elapsed, remove all food bowls from the cage. Leave only water. During the daytime, the parrot will stay occupied taking care of itself and playing with toys.

Parrots have a crop which is like a pocket for food in the neck. So, don't worry, your bird will continue processing that food throughout the day.

In the evening, you will have a second opportunity to take your parrot out of the cage, interact, do some training, and return the parrot back to the cage for the evening meal. Again, the parrot will have out of cage time and treats to look forward to for coming out and a meal for going back in.

Quite often, parrots are not fans of eating vegetables or healthy foods in general. You can put all the healthiest foods in front of your parrot, but they will serve no benefit unless the parrot actually eats them. A good strategy to encourage a parrot to actually consume healthier foods is to offer them exclusively at every fourth meal. For example, Monday morning feeding is pellets, Monday evening is pellets, Tuesday morning is pellets, but Tuesday evening is a bowl of just broccoli. The bird is more likely to form healthy eating habits. This teaches the parrot to accept and consume healthier foods and makes it less picky in the future.

Following this healthy feeding schedule will ensure that your parrot is both eating healthier and is in a healthy mindset for training.

Clicker Conditioning

A clicker is an amazing tool for teaching tricks and good behavior to parrots. The clicker itself is a plastic box that when pressed makes a click sound. The concept is amazingly simple while the results are absolutely brilliant. When an animal does what the trainer wants, or something that closely approximates this, the trainer clicks the clicker and then provides a reward. The clicker serves as a communication bridge to help mark to the animal with precision the moment that it executed the wanted behavior that is being rewarded, thus encouraging the behavior to repeat (remember positive reinforcement?).

The reason that using such a bridge is beneficial to training is that it provides a consistent and repeatable mechanism for the parrot to learn that the behavior at the moment of the sound is the one to strive for. Without the clicker bridge, the parrot would have to guess which of the many things prior to receiving a treat was the one that earns it treats. Another advantage of using a clicker is that over time it becomes a conditioned secondary reinforcer. In other words the parrot becomes so accustomed to striving to earn treats through clicks, that even the clicks themselves become a modest reward that can occasionally be used in place of food treats.

Some trainers and many private owners prefer to use a verbal bridge such as saying "good." However, in my experience a clicker is superior because it is more time specific, more pronounced, cannot be confused with normal speech, and most importantly can be used by other people to achieve results with your parrot. There are many different ways the word can be said and one person's "good" is not someone else's "gewd." No matter who wields the clicker, the parrot knows that it did the right thing and can trust this person to give treats in return for proper behavior.

Personally, I also like to offer verbal praise to my parrots in addition to the clicker because verbal praise is something I can use even when I don't have a clicker on hand. Thus, I take advantage of both methods but mainly rely on the clicker while allowing verbal praise to become another backup reinforcer.

During at least the first six months of training and possibly forever, a food reward should be offered as soon as possible after a click of the clicker. Make sure you have a treat ready in advance so that you can give it right after the click. Eventually, it is possible to use a clicker for every correct behavior but then offer treats on an intermittent basis. There will be more information about this in a later chapter but until you have extensive success with clicker training, stick to one-click one-treat to ensure you are doing it properly.

Remember that a parrot does not come with an inherent awareness of what a click is, so the first stage of training is to teach it that click means a treat is on the way. To teach this, go up to your parrot and begin handing out treats. If the parrot is already tame, you can do this out of the cage. If it is not, leave it in the cage and offer treats from your hand through the bars.

It is best to do this clicker conditioning prior to meal times so that the parrot is hungriest and these clicks/treats are most memorable.

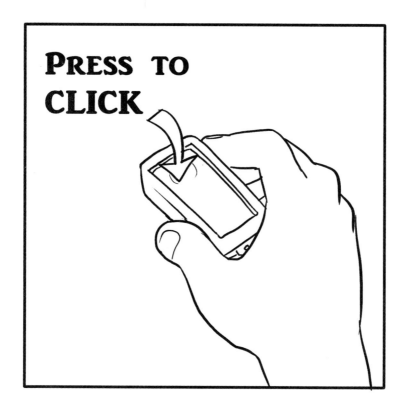

As you continue giving treats to your parrot, begin to use the clicker. Oftentimes the clicker can be a bit startling to a new parrot, so a good way to reduce the impact of the sound is to hold the clicker behind your back while offering treats with your other hand. As the parrot becomes less startled by the sound, use the clicker closer and in sight. Remember to click exactly once while handing a treat to the parrot. Continue handing out treats and gradually begin to click just before offering the treat.

To make your clicker sessions more productive, lure the parrot to walk some distances in order to get the treat. For example, click and offer a treat on one side of the perch or cage, then next time click and have the parrot walk to the other side for the next one. Not only does this continue the clicker training but also prepares the parrot for the next stage of training. In this process, the parrot is learning to make an effort to get treats rather than just having them placed in its beak.

While you continue the clicker conditioning process, this is a good time to get in the habit of using the clicker efficiently. At first you can hold the clicker any way you feel comfortable but as you progress, try to hold it concealed in your hand while using your middle or ring finger to squeeze the clicker (refer to figure on page 106, photo page 293). This will free up other fingers for holding treats or directing the parrot in further training. Try to practice holding the clicker and treat in the same hand, click, and then give the treat to the parrot. At first, this is hard to do but with a little practice and exercise it will become very easy and will prepare you for future stages of training. This may seem a bit cumbersome at first but don't give up. While your parrot learns, you learn as well. It's a good idea to practice this ahead of time away from your parrot to ensure you're doing it right when it matters.

A final note about using the clicker, make sure that the parrot always gets a treat while hearing a click or shortly after. If you happen to drop the treat or couldn't get it to the parrot in time, try to have a spare treat nearby to use. If too much time went by though, forget the botched attempt and just click again when you are ready to give the next treat.

For most parrots, 3 sessions with about 10-20 small treats will be enough to learn to associate the clicker with food. You will be able to tell that the parrot has learned the clicker concept when you can make the click sound with no food in sight and the parrot, out of habit, is already looking for where you normally offer food. Once you have reached this stage, move on with training. You don't want to get the parrot too used to getting treats for nothing so there is no point continuing this clicker conditioning stage any more than necessary. Even if things move slowly, don't spend more than 5 sessions for training the clicker. If the parrot doesn't get it now, it will eventually pick it up while learning in the targeting stage.

Target Training

Targeting is one of the most useful skills a companion parrot can learn and is also one of the most successful methods for reducing biting problems. The purpose of targeting is to show a parrot where to go and what to touch.

Typically, you use a target stick for target training. If you don't have one, a chopstick (such as from an Asian restaurant) works well. Alternatively, a wooden dowel or other safe wooden stick can be used. Avoid using pencils, pens, or anything that can be dangerous to your parrot if ingested. A stick with a narrow point is ideal because it narrows down the parrots touch to a very specific place and not just a broad area. This will be useful later on for teaching the parrot to touch very specific things.

Some parrots will be fearful of the stick while others may get aggressive and try to tear it to pieces. Don't worry because there are solutions for these issues but keep some spare sticks handy if your bird is a big chewer. For an already tame parrot that will step up, you will have quickest results by practicing this outside the cage on a training perch (photo on page 295). For parrots that cannot be easily picked up, you can follow the same process inside the cage, but it may take a little longer to succeed.

Remind the parrot that clicker equals treats by clicking and rewarding a few times. Now you can introduce the target concept. In one hand hold the clicker and a treat. In the other, hold just the target stick. Bring the target stick up to your parrot's beak but stop about 1/4" away so that the stick is in easy reach but not touching. Luckily, most parrots have the habit of touching/biting stuff that comes in front of their beak, so it is very likely that your parrot will make a move at the stick. When it does, click the moment it comes in contact with the target stick, withdraw the stick, and give the treat.

If your parrot is not afraid of the stick but doesn't make any effort to touch it, keep holding it a while longer and see if it eventually does. You can try withdrawing the stick and approaching again. If this still fails, you can try touching the tip of the stick to the tip of your parrot's beak, click, and reward. Repeat this a few times and see if the parrot got it and makes the effort to reach toward and touch the stick by itself next time. If this is still failing, you can try to set the stick so that it is in the parrot's way when it is walking so that it inadvertently bumps into it gently and then click/reward. The point is to find ways for the parrot to end up touching the stick on its own so that it can learn that this is the purpose. Continuing to touch the stick to the parrot's beak yourself more than a few times to get started will end up teaching the parrot to sit and be touched rather than what is needed.

Now if your parrot is afraid of the target stick all together, don't go chasing after the parrot with the stick. Instead, hold the tip of the stick at some distance from the parrot such that the parrot is unbothered. Now you will need a lot of patience and possibly repeat sessions. If the parrot makes any movement in the direction of the target stick, even if it is as little as turning its head in that direction, click and reward. If the parrot moves away from the stick, do nothing and keep waiting for it to eventually move toward the stick. Progressively reduce the distance to the stick and continue providing rewards for when the parrot moves toward the stick. Eventually the parrot will no longer be afraid of the target stick and you will be able to apply the previously mentioned methods of getting it to touch and move on from there.

After the first few times that your parrot touches the target stick for the treat, it is already time to move on and challenge the parrot more. You never want to withhold progress by insufficiently challenging your parrot. Instead, if you always try to get the bird to do more, you will ultimately have much greater success. Start holding the target stick at slightly longer distances. First, a quarter inch, then a half, then a whole inch. Point the target stick to the side of your parrot's head so that it can turn its head and touch it. Don't get too hasty if the parrot is not touching the stick. Try to wait it out and see if it will eventually turn and touch. If, however, within 30 seconds of presenting the stick the parrot still does not touch, take the target stick away, wait 15-30 seconds, then offer it again but slightly closer/easier than previously. Once you can get your parrot to turn its head a few times to touch the stick, try from the other side. Then try holding the target stick just so far that the parrot has to stretch for it. Always click and reward when it touches the stick. Continue challenging your parrot to take a step to touch and then a few. Just keep stretching the distance with successive attempts.

Within a few training sessions like this you will be able to target your parrot to either end of a perch and eventually all around the cage. You can further challenge your parrot and give it more exercise by making it walk to the target stick but then walk some more for the treat. For example, target your parrot to the furthest end of the cage but then hold the treat to the other side so that the parrot has to walk/climb back to get the food. Be careful not to turn the targeting exercise into a dance of walking to one side to touch and back for treat. Keep mixing up where you make the parrot go so that it learns specifically to go wherever the stick is and not to just walk back and forth on a perch.

Limit target training sessions to about 10-20 times using small treats for each touch. End the session before the parrot has a chance to get full or bored. Try to end sessions on a good note when you are achieving success and improvement. Use smaller treats during the repetitive bits. Give a bigger treat (such as sunflower seed, almond, or piece of fruit) for a very successful improvement or for the last target in the session. It's a good idea to say "target" or "touch" every time you present the target stick. This will tell the parrot what you are asking for and is a helpful reminder when it is confused. Furthermore, this will prepare the parrot to learn cues you may use in the future for tricks or just good behavior. Lastly, by knowing the word "touch," you can later apply it to other objects but with the same purpose. For example, if the parrot is afraid of a new toy, you can say touch and out of habit the parrot targets to it. Don't forget to click and reward to maintain consistency.

Here are a few more tips for target training. Never use the same stick that is meant for targeting for anything else including stepping onto. It is important to keep the target stick solely for the concept of targeting. Always make certain the parrot gets a click & treat whenever it touches the target stick. If you click accidentally, still give a treat. Never under any circumstances push, hit, or block the parrot using the target stick. The entire point of the target stick is to have something that is immaculately good and never bad. This is an object that the parrot can entirely trust. Hands are unpredictable because they could be used for doing good things to the parrot but they can also be used to grab or scare. The target stick must remain a device that is used for nothing but providing treats in return for touching.

If your parrot bites hard on the stick, there is a simple solution for teaching it to be more gentle. Simply click the clicker a little earlier. Click as the parrot's beak is hovering over the stick but before it can bite down. Quickly withdraw the stick to avoid the bite while simultaneously bringing the treat over. The parrot will soon learn that it only needs to come right up to and aim for the stick but not rip it to shreds. It's a bad idea to allow a parrot to attack the stick violently. Not only does this ruin your tool but can also lead the bird to behave this way toward fingers.

The biggest success in using target training is that it inadvertently teaches a parrot to cooperate instead of biting. The parrot learns that following this safe and easy procedure will get it something it wants while it is impossible for anything bad to happen. The beauty of targeting is that it can later be used to teach the parrot to step up onto hands, to become comfortable with things or people it is scared of, and to teach tricks. The target stick provides familiarity to a parrot in unfamiliar circumstances and helps transfer over the existing skill to novel situations. Over time, targeting also teaches a parrot not to bite, because all of the time spent engaged in the activity, is not spent biting. The two are mutually exclusive. The parrot develops a long term habit of doing something other than biting and thus biting follows a path of extinction because it does not occur. On the flip side, targeting is an easy hands off mechanism for the owner to teach the parrot not to bite without having to take any bites in the process. Both the owner and the parrot get to take their time getting used to each other in a rewarding way and without any pain in the process. When your parrot is good at targeting, you will be ready to move onto the next stage which is teaching the parrot to step up onto your hand by targeting.

Step Up

Whether your parrot is tame or not, knows how to step up or doesn't, it's a good idea to teach the bird to step up by targeting. The reason is that it creates a positive-reinforced behavior that will stick for life (as opposed to the negative reinforced means of teaching step up most commonly used) and it can be transferred to other people. Some day you may want a friend, relative, or new owner to be able to hold the parrot. If the parrot learned to step up by targeting for you, it will be quicker and easier to teach the bird to step up for someone else. As baby parrots grow up, they can often become resistant to cooperating the way they once did. Again, having a deliberately trained method for step up makes it easier to repair and rekindle. Teaching step up as outlined here, helps solve or prevent biting issues from occurring.

The step up training comes in three phases. First, targeting the parrot onto a handheld perch. Second, targeting the parrot onto your hand or finger. And third, just having the parrot step up. The key is to have the parrot step up voluntarily on its own every time. Do not just put your hand in front of the bird or force the bird onto your hand. This can lead to biting immediately or at other seemingly unrelated times. Training the parrot to step up ensures that the parrot comes onto the hand without biting and continues to stay on the hand without biting because it chose to be there. Tricking the parrot onto your hand, even if you avoid a bite for now, could still result in a bite later when the parrot regrets being on your hand. Just because a parrot stepped up earlier does not mean that this exact specific time it is willing or ready to step up. By giving the parrot a choice (while making that choice very enticing), we are able to eliminate the parrot needing to revert to undesirable behavior. Trained step up thus reduces/eliminates biting behavior in parrots.

Using the target stick during step up training is so effective because the parrot has already learned the concept and knows what to do. Better still is the fact that the parrot is focused on the stick and its beak is pointing at the stick, so there is much less chance that it will bite you in the process.

For this exercise, you will need a little coordination. You must be able to hold the clicker, target stick, and treat all in one hand (figure on page 106, photo on page 293). Tuck the clicker into your hand and click with middle or ring finger. Slide the target stick into your hand. It doesn't matter if you can't aim it with your fingers because you can just move your entire hand to position it. Finally, tuck the parrot's treat (or millet spray strand for parakeets) between your thumb and index finger so that you can quickly provide it. Don't lure the parrot with the treat in your fingers though. After clicking, turn your wrist to move the target stick away and make the treat accessible. It's a good idea to practice this one handed target exercise with your parrot a bunch of times prior to moving onto the next steps.

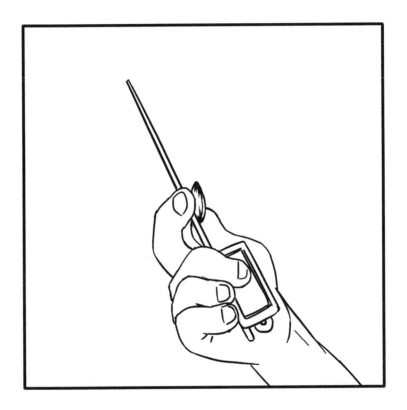

You will begin step up training with the aid of a handheld perch. You can remove a familiar perch from the parrot's cage to use for this exercise or purchase another perch that is similar.

If you are able to get your parrot out from the cage and onto a training perch, this will be the best place to perform the step up exercises. However, if you are unable to move your parrot without causing it stress, these exercises can be performed in the cage. Once enough training progress is made in the cage that you can take the parrot out comfortably, continue on a training perch for better focus.

Hold the clicker, target stick, and treat in one hand (dominant hand) and the handheld perch in the other. If the perch has a bolt for attaching to the cage, hold it on that side.

The parrot is either on a training perch or in the cage. Lean the tip of the handheld perch on the perch the parrot is on. Set it to the side of the parrot and no closer than 6 inches away. Once set, try not to move the handheld perch as you are trying to convince that this perch is nothing more than an extension of the perch the bird is already on (photo on page 294).

Do not bring the handheld perch directly up to the parrot. Instead, direct the parrot to walk to the handheld perch using your target stick. At first, the parrot may be hesitant to walk onto the handheld perch. This is alright. Targeting the parrot to come a little closer to the handheld perch is already a good start. Continue targeting the parrot closer and closer to the handheld perch. Click the clicker and give a treat whenever the parrot touches the target stick. Eventually, the parrot will come near the handheld perch to reach the target stick.

Hold the target stick above the handheld perch so that the parrot has to step onto the perch to reach the target. Do not ask for too much, but do challenge the parrot to venture a little further each time. After every successful target, let the parrot return to its original perch or target the parrot back to reset the exercise. It won't be much longer until the parrot will step one foot onto the handheld perch and eventually both.

Keep the parrot's attention on the target stick. This will prevent biting as the parrot's gaze and attention will be on the target stick rather than your hand. Furthermore, this helps teach the parrot to step up only using its feet. Oftentimes parrots revert to using their beak as a third hand while stepping up. This makes people nervous, especially those who are unfamiliar with the bird. Keep the parrot focused on the target stick to teach it to keep the beak high (and away from hands) while stepping up.

The parrot will soon be able to walk onto the handheld perch to touch the target stick. However, don't get too excited and take the parrot away on the handheld perch. Continue practicing this exercise some more so that the parrot does not lose trust in the handheld perch. If the parrot does not walk off the handheld perch by itself, you can target the parrot back to its original perch.

Once the parrot is reliably targeting onto the handheld perch, you are ready for the next step. Now you no longer have to lean the handheld perch onto the perch the parrot is on. Instead, hold the handheld perch next to the perch the parrot is on. Remember not to put the handheld perch directly in front of the parrot but always to the side. The parrot should have to take a few steps sideways before it can step up onto the handheld perch. Continue using the target stick to direct the parrot. The bird will learn to step onto a perch that is not completely steady.

After a bit more practice, you will be ready to start taking the bird around the room on the handheld perch. Do this in stages rather than all at once. Target the parrot onto the handheld perch, slowly move the handheld perch a few inches, and return the bird back to the original perch. Take the bird farther with each subsequent attempt. You will soon be ready to take the parrot between different bird stands in your home and to the training perch.

Once the bird is reliable at stepping onto the handheld perch, it is time to begin the transition to using your hand instead. Up to this point, the parrot has been developing a habit not only of stepping up but also not biting. Both you and your parrot have been developing trust in the process. Before you can have your parrot on your hand, you will need to transition from a long handheld perch to a shorter one. You will shorten the perch by hiding the excess under your hand. Slide the perch farther into your hand, leaving a shorter perch available for the parrot to step onto. As you continue to practice, the parrot will start getting used to stepping onto the perch in closer proximity to your hand. Keep the parrot's attention on the target stick to divert attention from your hand or from biting it.

The handheld perch will start to appear very short as you hold it closer and closer to where the parrot will step. With every successful step up, hold it a little closer to where the parrot will step. Soon, the parrot will run out of room and end up on your hand instead. For small parrots, hold your finger across the handheld perch. For medium parrots, do this with your hand. For large parrots, hold your entire arm across the handheld perch. In any case, the parrot will be stepping onto you while trying to get onto the perch that you are covering (photo on page 294). To prevent biting and to remind the parrot what to do, use the clicker, target stick, and treat the same as before.

Continue holding the handheld perch under your finger or arm a little while longer to serve as a reminder for the parrot. Soon, you will not need to hold the handheld perch any longer and simply target the parrot onto your finger, hand, or arm. Do not forget to set your hand steady **to the side** of the parrot and then target the parrot to walk toward your hand.

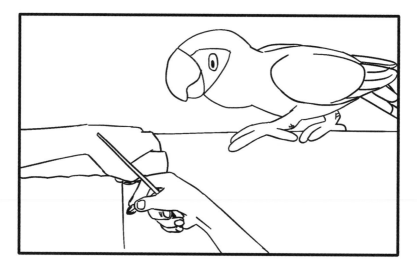

Now it is time to phase out the target stick. Just like the handheld perch, you can make the target stick shorter by hiding more of it in your hand (photo on page 293). Push the target stick farther into your fist each time you use it until the visible portion of the stick is tiny. It will continue to serve as a reminder for the parrot of what to do and where to point its beak.

The last step to phasing out the target stick is to start showing the already barely visible target stick farther away from the bird. In fact, you will hold the target stick far enough back that the parrot will never be able to reach it. Instead of saying "target," you can now begin saying "step up." And instead of clicking when the parrot touches the target stick, you can click once both of the parrot's feet are on your hand. This transition changes the goal from targeting to stepping up. The cue is different and the click happens for a different outcome. Now, you ask the parrot to step up and click the clicker for stepping up. A treat follows as usual. Continue showing the small target stick farther until you no longer need to show it at all. Simply present your finger, hand, or arm from the side of the parrot and say "step up." Wait for the parrot to walk toward your hand and step on it. Once the parrot places its second foot onto your hand, click & reward.

Repeat the entire step up training with your other hand. Many times parrots get too accustomed only to stepping on a particular hand. It is best to repeat the entire training on the other hand, but it will go quicker this time. For every other person in the household that wishes to handle the parrot, repeat the step up training as well.

Practice having your parrot come over and step up onto your hand from different places. Turn it into a game by having your parrot step up from one place to be carried to the next. Have the parrot step up from the cage, place the parrot on a tree stand, then have the parrot step up and place the parrot on a training perch and so on. Be sure to click and give a treat after every step up so that strong habits will form.

MEDIUM PARROT: HAND

Congratulations! Now you have taught your parrot to step up. Better still, you taught the parrot to step up voluntarily! Not only has the parrot learned to come onto the hand, it has learned to want to be on the hand. The parrot that wants to be there has far less reason to bite than a parrot that does not. Going forward, always show your hand to the side of the parrot and leave enough room for your parrot to make a few steps. Continue using the clicker for a few more weeks, but eventually phase it out. However, continue giving a treat every time your parrot steps up for the span of a year to develop maximum reliability. As you teach your parrot tricks and flight recall, the parrot will begin to have other incentives to step up. Instead of receiving treats directly for stepping up, the parrot will need to step up to participate in other activities that earn it treats.

Always treat step up as a request rather than a command. Ask the parrot to step up by showing your hand to the side. If the parrot agrees, it will walk over and get onto your hand. If it is unwilling, it will stay where it stands. This eliminates the tendency for the parrot to bite to avoid stepping up. Accept this as constructive feedback and try harder to offer the bird a compelling reason to come to your hand. Teaching and maintaining reliable step up is essential for having a well-behaved parrot. Respecting the parrot's free will and making step up worthwhile is the foundation of having a successful bird-human relationship.

Touch/Grab

Since this chapter is about the basics of parrot taming and training, I will continue to describe how to tame a parrot to allow you to touch and eventually grab it. However, you should continue teaching tricks and flight (if applicable) as described later on in the book simultaneously. You see this taming process takes substantially longer than training. You will sooner see results from training. It is important to get a head start on this taming process early so that by the time your parrot is learning tricks it is already becoming tamer as well.

Being able to touch and grab your parrot is not just something that would be nice to do with your pet, it is actually necessary. First of all, it is necessary because for practical and safety reasons there will be times when you will have to. But more importantly, it will gain greater trust and reduce biting. If your parrot is willing or better yet thrilled to get grabbed by you, then it won't ever bite to try to prevent you from touching or holding it. A lot of unexpected biting has to do with the fact that the parrot is trying to avoid stepping up or being held, yet if this is always an enjoyable experience, then this type of biting is automatically mitigated.

The process begins by taking the parrot out of the cage using the step up technique and placing it on a training perch out of sight of the cage. It is always better to train away from the cage to avoid interference from territory issues or distraction from cage stuff. Use a perch without toys or places to go. I recommend my line of Parrot Training Perches from the ParrotWizard.com store as an ideal training aid. The stands are simple and height is adjustable. A quick and dirty option is to set your parrot on top of a chair back (like a kitchen chair). Ideally, the parrot should be on a perch that puts the parrot's head just below your chin.

Do not use a clicker for the hand taming and grab exercises. The clicker is best used for training when the parrot is being taught a specific action. In this case, the parrot is being taught to do nothing and allow the hand to approach. There is no specific moment of correct behavior to be able to click for.

Begin the touch taming process by hovering your open hand a few feet away from above and to the side of the parrot at about a 45 degree angle (figure on page 117, photo on page 296). If the parrot is very hand skittish, you may have to start this from even further away. Begin at a distance where the parrot simply does not react or care about the presence of your hand. If it is trying to bite, cower, or shake, then your hand is too close and in this case start further away. Likewise, if your parrot is happy to see your hand, asks for a head scratch, or tries to approach, this is still undesirable. The goal is to show the hand so far away that it elicits nothing more than complete indifference. This is the behavior we are trying to teach so that hands can approach.

Approach slowly with your hand to avoid startling the parrot or even drawing attention. Stop at a distance, give a treat, and then remove your hand. Repeat this progressively closer and closer. Make sure that you never breach your parrot's comfort zone. It's better to do this process too slowly and never tempt it to bite than to go too fast and let it try to bite. The more experiences you share with your parrot that do not tempt it to bite, the less likely the parrot considers biting as an option.

You will continue to progress closer and closer until you are just outside of the parrot's bite range. This is the distance that if you put your hand any closer, the parrot could stretch and reach the hand to bite. Before continuing to practice this exercise any closer, and within biting reach, stop and work on a few other skills.

Work on increasing duration that the parrot stays calm in the presence of the hovering hand by giving several treats in a row before removing the hand. Teach patience further by offering the treats more slowly. Have your treat hand move toward the parrot in slow motion so that the parrot knows a treat is coming but has to stay in the presence of the hovering hand for longer. Lastly, try to encourage more still behavior. After all, you are not only teaching the parrot to allow you to touch but also teaching a "stay" command while you are touching. Reward the parrot when it is more calm and sometimes do not reward the parrot when it is more fidgety.

Now, with the extra trust built of the closely hovering hand (while working on duration), you are finally ready to venture closer. Again, approach the hand at an angle from above and to the side. But now, you will ever so slightly approach at a distance where the parrot could (if it really wanted to and stretched) bite you. However, after so many times trusting your hand before, the parrot has no reason to distrust now. Reward and repeat. Continue to hover the hand closer each time. But, only a little closer. Do not rush to start touching. Eventually you will be hovering your hand an inch away, half an inch, and closer still.

At some point you will make gentle contact with the feathers on the head. Continue approaching closer still in subsequent tries. How can you get closer than touching? Apply slightly more and more pressure so that the parrot can feel the touch. Now you are able to touch the parrot on the head.

It is very important to repeat this exercise the same way with your opposite hand. Do not assume that because the parrot learned to trust one hand that it automatically trusts the other! However, since the parrot is familiar with the process, repeating this exercise from the other side should go more quickly. Also, make sure if any other person is going to be touching the parrot, that they do not assume your parrot's trust for your hands will carry over. Have every person that will be touching the parrot practice the same exercise.

For tamer birds this process may only take a few days. For skittish or biting parrots this can take weeks or months. This process must not be rushed and it is well worth the slow effort because of the good behavior that it ultimately encourages. It's good to mix in some target or trick training in the process and only do the hand taming process as a long term supplement. Don't forget to work on the taming every day but limit to 5-10 times per session. This process is inevitably slower than training because it is mainly a factor of the parrot becoming familiar with you and overcoming fear.

You can even sneak some more taming amid training. For example, when you continue practicing targeting with your parrot, you can hover your hand in a similar manner whenever it is eating a treat that it earned through targeting. Also mix in some intentional hand hovers between targeting.

Keep practicing this method until you are able to cup your parrot from above with your hand. In the process the parrot is learning to stay still and not bite. If your parrot moves while you are trying to touch or cup it, take your hand away and ignore it. You are thus able to discourage your parrot for not cooperating by not giving it the treat it has come to expect from you. Give it another chance. If the parrot is still too fidgety, consider ending the session. If this is a long term issue, then reward the times the bird is more still but not the ones when it walks too far. You may need to move back to the hover method for a bit before moving back to touch.

Continue using this approach until you are able to touch your parrot both on its back and its head. You will eventually be able to use head touching to teach petting to the parrot and back cupping to be able to grab the bird. As you do more practice of cupping your hand around the parrot, begin to apply an upward lifting force. For a macaw you may need to use both hands to continue the grab training but for smaller birds you can continue with one hand. Keep increasing the duration of back cupping and lifting the bird higher (and of course rewarding after) until you can lift the parrot so its feet leave the perch. If the parrot is cooperating but holding onto the perch too firmly, you can try to get it to let go by reaching your other hand in like for a step up. When the parrot releases the perch, don't let it step up but put treats into its beak while it is held above the perch by your hand.

At this point you are able to pick up your parrot, so all that is left is making it completely routine. What you don't want to do is just pick up and hold your parrot for a long time because as it gets bored, tired, or uncomfortable, it may bite. Instead, get the bird involved in things so it stays preoccupied. Grab the parrot from one training perch and set it on another. Slowly spread the distance between the training perches. This allows the parrot to predict that it will be placed down soon.

Grab the bird and carry it to the other end of the room. Grab it and put it on your hand. Grab it, put a treat in its beak and put it back down. Grab it and put it back in the cage. Grab it out of the cage, give it a treat and stick it back in the cage. You see the possibilities are vast. By mixing it up and giving treats less frequently on a random basis, the bird will learn to just chill when you reach to grab it.

Continue getting the parrot comfortable being grabbed by different hands and different ways. Remember never to squeeze the belly because birds don't have a diaphragm and must be able to move their chest to breath. The optimal way to grab a parrot for the purpose of carrying it is by the neck from above and then to roll it on its back to lay on your hand (refer to figure on page 125). With larger parrots it may require two hands and with smaller ones just fingers. The idea is still the

same though. It is safer to hold a parrot by its neck than by its belly. It also develops a means of restraint that can be used during grooming or medical procedures. When a parrot is accustomed that most times it is grabbed, outcomes are positive or at least neutral, the few bad experiences (like medicating or grooming) will be canceled out. But if you wait to do grab training till you really need it, the bad experiences, being primal, will far outweigh the good ones and it will be hard to get near the parrot to begin the training. Don't wait. Take the time to do it right and do it early.

Toweling

Like grab, I think it is better to teach toweling in a no-pressure good atmosphere and not wait until it is necessary. Ultimately, I think grab training is far more useful, but just to ensure your parrot doesn't get scared of towels when needed, perform this taming ahead of time as well. What I am definitely against is just forcing a towel on a parrot. The old school approach was to just grab a parrot in a towel and hold it for a very long time until it gives up the struggle. That process is called flooding and while it may seem effective, it is far more detrimental to your relationship. Flooding may also lead to random biting in fear that the towel may be used. By solving one problem, a far bigger problem is created. Thus a positive reinforcement based approach is much better suited.

If your parrot has never seen a towel before or is already towel neutral, this will be very easy. If your parrot is scared of the towel, I will also describe a procedure for overcoming this. Start by finding an appropriately sized towel. Don't use a beach towel on a cockatiel or a wash cloth on a macaw. Find a towel that will fully envelope the parrot without much excess. With your parrot on a training perch, chair back, or other uninhibited location, show the towel from a distance. Demonstrate the towel from different sides, wrap your own arm in it, play with the material to show the parrot that the towel in itself is harmless.

Slowly walk closer to the parrot and display the towel two feet away and give a treat. Show the towel from a closer distance and reward. Continue reducing the distance until you can touch the parrot with just the tip of it. To make the towel less threatening, hold just a small piece reaching above your hand and the rest dangling below. At first, use that short corner sticking out from your hand but progressively show more. If the parrot gets scared by backing away or flying away, you must take things much slower. Definitely don't let things get to the point where the parrot tries to bite. If you have reached your parrot's comfort threshold, continue practicing with the towel no closer than that distance and give treats every time you approach with it. Take the towel further away and then reach in closer again with treat in hand. You can cheat a little by simultaneously moving both the towel and the hand with the treat closer. Have the treat aimed at the parrot's beak so that it is distracted by the treat and allows the towel closer. Getting to the point of touching the parrot may take a few iterations or possibly days. Continue working at your parrot's pace.

Touch the parrot with more and more of the towel during successive attempts. Ideally, the parrot should already be comfortable with the grab procedure, so what you can begin to do is drape some towel material over the bird (but not the whole towel) and grabbing it through the towel. Reward with treats and praise. Keep practicing until you can drape the towel around the bird and grab it. Most parrots tend to get cuddly around soft things like towels so you can turn this into a game of peekaboo or just petting. To maintain comfort with towels in the long run, you can use a towel to dry off your parrot (by wrapping or dabbing, don't rub) after a shower. Since the bird is cold with water, being wrapped in a warm towel will feel good and automatically reinforce the experience.

Turning on Back

The last bit of simple yet important taming is being able to flip the parrot on its back. It may not serve a specific purpose but it just anchors the level of trust in people's hands. When the bird is comfortable with you touching, grabbing, holding, and putting it on its back, it has nothing to fear. This type of training creates the ultimate level of trust. To tame your parrot to allow you to turn it on its back, it must already be very comfortable with being grabbed. Make sure your parrot has been familiar with grab for a while (at least 1-2 weeks) before you roll it on its back or the parrot may revert to distrusting grab in the process.

With your parrot perching on one hand, cup your parrot's back (or grab its neck from behind). Release and give a reward. Do this a few times to get it used to the exercise. Now begin to tilt the bird by slowly rotating it back. Start with very small amounts at first. Never just jump to turning the bird all the way. Tilt the bird maybe just 10 degrees. Don't wait for it to get uncomfortable, upright the parrot and give a reward. Continue this procedure with slow increments of greater tilt until the parrot is turned 90 degrees and laying on your cupping hand. Remember to have treats prepared and laid out in advance to avoid a long delay between behavior and reward.

All that is left is to get the bird to release its grip on the hand it is perching on. If you can wiggle that hand loose, continue holding the bird with your other hand. Quickly grab a treat and put it in its beak before you upright it. If the bird has a killer grip on your hand and absolutely won't let go, you can use the already known *grab* and rotate it with the one hand without any perching. Simply grab the bird, pick it up off your hand or perch. Roll it back to the extent to which it is comfortable. Use your free hand to stick a treat in its beak and then upright it. Eventually, you will be able to just grab, tilt on its back, hold, and reward the parrot. This will be useful for carrying the bird around or working on tricks (photo on page 299). It also helps make for a cuddle bug of a parrot.

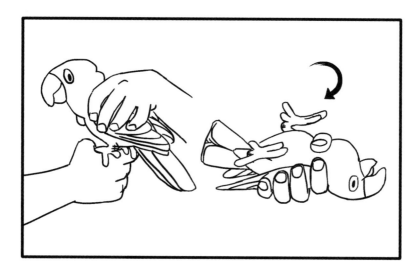

Congratulations! You are on your way to having a well-behaved parrot. Understanding the basics of taming and training and teaching them to the parrot is where it all begins. Having a parrot on a healthy feeding plan that is motivated for training is key to success. Patience, practice, and perseverance will convert little successes into long term behavior. You are on your way to a well-rounded and well-behaved parrot!

Chapter 4 Checklist:

- ❏ Set up a distraction free training area
- ❏ Configure a Parrot Training Perch for focused training
- ❏ Adjust perch height (parrot's head below your chin)
- ❏ Establish a training schedule in mornings and/or evenings
- ❏ Quit while you're ahead when training is going well
- ❏ Use positive reinforcement (give treats to increase behavior)
- ❏ Avoid deliberate or inadvertent use of punishment
- ❏ Use prevention to avoid undesirable behavior
- ❏ Establish training motivation and prepare treats
- ❏ Follow a healthy feeding plan
- ❏ Determine what you feed, how you feed, when you feed, and how much you feed for healthy feeding
- ❏ Feed healthy meals in the morning and evening
- ❏ Remove food from cage outside of meal times
- ❏ Practice training prior to meals
- ❏ Introduce clicker and practice clicker conditioning
- ❏ Start target training in the cage or on a training perch
- ❏ Get the parrot to reliably follow the target stick for treats
- ❏ Always ask a parrot to step up by showing your hand from the side and not in front of the bird
- ❏ Use a handheld perch, clicker, target stick, and treats to train step-up using positive reinforcement
- ❏ Phase out the handheld perch, target, clicker, and treats
- ❏ Practice hand taming by hovering your hand
- ❏ Reward indifferent reaction and staying still for hand taming
- ❏ Extend process to grab training
- ❏ Use similar process for toweling
- ❏ Practice turning parrot on back in small increments

Chapter 5: Managing Good Behavior

Good behavior should not be taken for granted. It doesn't come hardwired in a parrot because what we consider good behavior may be bad for survival in the wild. Meanwhile the things that are necessary for survival in the wild are often very troublesome in the home. The idea is to encourage more of the desirable behavior so that it can take place of unsuitable behavior. Although it is impossible to eliminate all unwanted natural behaviors in parrots, it is important to avoid encouraging them to happen any more than the absolute minimum.

Routine and habit play a large role in the ways our parrots behave. If they are never given the opportunity or temptation to bite, they rarely think of resorting to biting. On the flip side, the more often a parrot naturally resorts to biting, the sooner it will employ this technique again even when unnecessary. It is necessary to set up good habits, routine, and success all around.

While focused training sessions may be necessary to teach certain behaviors initially, in the long run a lot of the basic behavior can be maintained without clicker or treats. This does not mean that the behavior no longer needs to be positively reinforced, however, the reinforcement can become so faint and subtle that you wouldn't think of it as a reward. For long term behavior maintenance, alternative methods of reinforcement can be used, such as attention, petting, out of cage time, toys, and scheduled meals.

If you configure your routine similar to the suggestions to come, your parrot will inevitably continue receiving the positive reinforcement necessary to continue its good behavior but with less effort on your part. The only effort required is setting up and continuing the routine.

Step Up to Come Out of Cage

The most pleasant common parrot behavior for bird owners is having the parrot step up to come out of the cage. Without this, a companion parrot would be little more than a feathered fish in an aquarium. But unlike fish, parrots are highly social, intelligent, and capable of companionship with their human. In order to teach a parrot to step up to come out of the cage to begin with, refer to Chapter 4 regarding target training and step up training. Once the bird is good at stepping up in return for treats, other forms of reinforcement can be applied to make stepping up more frequent and easy to use.

Getting a parrot to step up onto your hand to come out of the cage without the need for a treat depends on two things. First of all, the parrot must already know how to and be willing to step up for a treat in training. Secondly, the parrot needs to want to be out of the cage. This is really the most fundamental part. If the parrot enjoys spending time out of the cage, the rest is just mechanics. By following the complete approach outlined in this book, your parrot will already have reasons to want to be out of the cage. Even if for no other reason, it will learn to want to be out of the cage just for the opportunity to train and earn treats. Over time the bird will become accustomed to your companionship and that alone will be enough to make it want to come out.

By following the healthy feeding schedule of two to three feedings a day, the parrot will look forward to coming out and having the chance to earn treats during training. Use the fact that the parrot wants to come out to your credit. Don't just open the door and allow the parrot to climb out on its own. Instead, ask it to walk over to your hand and step up. This way, the parrot will learn that you are the means by which it gets to come out and step up will be further reinforced without the use of treats. Using this method you will get to practice the "step up" concept several times a day without the use of treats and maintain this good behavior for life.

You can make coming out of the cage even easier by teaching the parrot to come to a perch by the door. Start by mounting a perch near the cage door but not actually on it. For about a week, target the parrot to that perch for a treat. And then have the parrot step up on your hand to come out. You can use a verbal cue such as "do you want to come out?" when you have the parrot come to that perch. It won't be long until your parrot climbs down to that perch when it sees you to ask to come out. If the parrot does not come to the perch on its own, you can ask, "do you want to come out?" and that may trigger the parrot to come.

If you are asking the parrot to come to the perch to come out and the parrot (that normally is good at this) does not, it may be an indication that the parrot would prefer to be left alone this time. When the parrot is 90%+ reliable at stepping up and coming to the perch by the door, it may well be exhibiting its preference. If the parrot is not eager to come out, avoid forcing it out, as you may find a higher likelihood of misbehavior or biting once the bird is out. If the parrot is not normally reliable at coming out, this may be a lack of training rather than an expression of its will. In that case, continue practicing the step up training and the coming out training until reliability is good.

Putting Parrot Back in Cage

Putting the parrot back in the cage may present a greater challenge than coming out if it enjoys being out. For many owners, getting the parrot out is easy but then putting it away is a nightmare. This is because they establish an imbalance of value between being out of cage and in. They provide ample food, toys, and entertainment for the parrot when it is out. The cage offers the same things but in a confined space. It's obvious that the parrot would rather be out of the cage than in it. What is not obvious is that the parrot can develop a habit of biting the owner instead of stepping up because of this. What happens is the parrot fears that anytime a hand approaches, it will be used to put the parrot back in the cage. So, the parrot preemptively bites to prevent this from happening. This might not be in proximity of the cage or even for the purpose of putting the parrot away, but the parrot gets aggressive toward hands anyway as a result.

In order to get a parrot to go back into the cage without any adverse side effects to the relationship, it is imperative that the parrot wants or better yet looks forward to going back into the cage. What could a parrot possibly like about being in the cage more than being out? Food. If you feed meals exclusively in the cage, going back into the cage is just like going home for dinner. If the parrot always gets to eat out, there is no advantage to going back in. But if there is no food (except treats for training) anywhere but the cage, the bird will gladly go back into the cage to accept its meal. Don't forget to have the meal in place inside the cage before putting the bird in. But, make sure the cage door stays closed and the bird can't just go in on its own. You should always have your bird step up or accept being grabbed by you to be put back into the cage. This is free and routine training that you must continue in order to avoid losing and having to retrain this behavior.

Initially, you can use target training and treats to practice having the parrot step up to go into or out of the cage. However, once you have the routine established, following the healthy feeding schedule automatically makes going back into the cage rewarding. If you feed the parrot only during scheduled meals, remove food in between, take the parrot out prior to its meal times, and then put it back in to an awaiting meal, both the problem of getting the parrot out of the cage and back into the cage is solved! You won't ever have to give the bird a treat or any other reason to go in or out simply by maintaining this schedule.

Weighing

Keeping track of your parrot's weight is an important part of monitoring your parrot's health. Parrots hide visible signs of illness, but discovering weight loss early on can be a strong indicator. If you weigh your parrot daily, you will be able to catch this and seek medical attention in time. For the purpose of healthy feeding, weighing the parrot allows you to keep track of the relationship between what you feed, how much you feed, the parrot's condition, and the parrot's motivation.

Training motivation correlates to the parrot's feeding and weight. Many parrots suffer health problems, such as fatty liver disease and atherosclerosis, as the result of obesity in captivity. When the parrot is at an unhealthy weight, training motivation will suffer. If a parrot's training motivation is inadequate, you can try replacing pellets/grains with more veggies in the diet or reduce meal size and body weight by up to 10%. A motivated parrot is more likely to be healthy both physically and mentally.

Temperature, daylight, and other seasonal changes can affect the parrot's calorie consumption and thus change its food portion requirements. Therefore, staying in touch with the bird's weight is helpful.

Ideally, purchase a scale with an integrated perch. This will make weighing your parrot a breeze. Alternatively, you can either weigh the parrot directly on the scale top or tare the scale with a perch standing on it. Use your clicker and target stick to encourage the parrot to step from your hand to the scale on its own. Incorporate this into your daily routine for it to become automatic.

The best time to weigh a parrot is in the morning after its big morning poop. This is usually the lowest weight that a parrot will reach throughout the day. Then if possible, weigh it again after its meal to learn its weight range. If a parrot weighed 150g before the meal and 160g after the meal, you would learn that the parrot consumed 10g of food and water during the meal. Weighing the parrot consistently helps cancel out the weight of food/water going through its system so you can focus on body mass weight. If your parrot is determined to be overweight and needs a reduction, it should be based on the lower morning weight.

It's a good idea to keep a chart of your parrot's weight to be familiar with maximum weight, minimum weight, and trends. If you make no portion adjustments, yet the bird loses 5% of its body weight, you should be concerned. If you notice over 10% unexplained weight loss, you should be making immediate arrangements with an avian vet.

Petting

Humans adore cute cuddly animals that melt away in their hands and want this from parrots as well. This may not be a natural bird behavior but is something birds can learn. And, once they realize they like it, they will keep begging for more.

Some parrots will already be used to it or may be naturally cuddly. With these, you don't have to do much besides enjoy. However, it is very important not to let the parrot become demanding. For all other parrots, here is the method to teach them to accept cuddling and petting. Essentially, it is a continuation of the grab training outlined in Chapter 4. Touch your parrot on the head and give a treat. Progress to touching the parrot in more places, for longer durations, for smaller and fewer treats. Eventually, you will be able to stroke your parrot's feathers but continue offering treats a while longer.

The great thing about teaching a parrot to accept petting in this way is that it will learn how to accept it and at the same time develop a double appreciation of it. The parrot will learn to enjoy this form of touching because it is associated with treats, but more importantly, the bird will realize that this feels nice. Once the parrot begins to directly enjoy it, treats will no longer be necessary. Eventually, when the parrot asks for petting, you will even be able to use it as a reward in place of food treats at times.

The way that most parrots prefer to be stroked is on the head and opposite the feathers. In other words, run your fingers above the head from back to front. They especially enjoy scratches around their ears (yes, they have ears but they are covered with feathers) and neck. When your parrot goes through a molt, it will regrow new pin feathers that it will particularly enjoy you scratching to open. These feel like pins and are not yet opened. Don't handle short pin feathers but once they are as long as surrounding feathers and feel flaky, you can roll and rub them between your fingers to break the sheath and let the new feather out. Birds naturally do this for each other, so a special bond is formed when you do this allopreening process for your parrot.

One last thing that is important to teach along with this kind of handling is petting etiquette. Left to its own ways, the parrot will bite to ask for petting, bite if you stop, bite if it wants more, bite if it wants no more, etc. Biting is the last thing you want during a cuddle session so here is a simple technique for teaching your parrot to communicate with you. Once your parrot is used to and enjoys petting, begin to tilt its head downward while you scratch. If you can, have the parrot stand on your hand and tilt its head between the fingers (of the hand it is standing on) and hold its beak. Meanwhile, continue petting with the other hand. This is useful in three ways. First, it gives you a bit of protection from bossy biting. The parrot can't bite you when you are already holding its beak. When it pulls away, you have time to react and this becomes the signal that it wants no more so that you don't force unwanted petting onto the bird either. Next, this creates a signal for when the bird wants head scratches. You'll be thrilled when your parrot just flies onto your hand, tilts its head, and slips its beak between your fingers begging you for a scratch. You won't be able to resist! Lastly, this is a safe way to allow strangers to pet your parrot (especially children). You can't take a chance of your parrot biting someone else, so by restraining its beak you ensure that the bird can't bite or will bite you first. Thus, you can signal to your parrot that petting is coming and your parrot has a means of asking for it.

  All biting must be ignored at the time of the bite. If you change what you are doing in response to a bite, it will tell the parrot that when it wants that action, to bite you. If you are not petting your parrot and it bites you and you begin to, it will learn to demand petting by biting. If you are already petting your parrot, it bites, and you stop, then it will learn to make you stop by biting. No matter what the consequence, any reaction to biting will only encourage it. Instead, learn what kinds of petting your parrot does and does not like, use the beak holding technique, do not force pet your parrot more than it would like, and keep it fun.

Shouldering

Everyone wants to be a pirate with a parrot on their shoulder. Likewise, most parrots want to be the parrot on the pirate's shoulder. But why do you think most pirates have eye patches? Keeping a misbehaving parrot on your shoulder is just asking for trouble. It is possible to receive a very serious injury from a biting parrot on your shoulder, so it is very important to have the right relationship before ever allowing the bird to be on there.

The reason I wrote "allowing" and not putting your parrot on your shoulder is because many parrots will run up your arm or fly straight to your shoulder on their own. Just not putting it there is not always enough as the parrot may quite well do it on its own. Until your parrot is an ace at stepping up and being grabbed, don't even think about letting it on your shoulder. What often happens is that the parrot eagerly gets on the shoulder but then starts biting any hand trying to remove it. Hey, if the parrot likes being there, then being taken off must be seen as a bad thing. The best way to avoid this sticky parrot syndrome is to prevent it from going on your shoulder until you can reliably have it step on and off of any other place.

Another major issue is that parrots on shoulders tend to get bored. And when they get bored they start playing with whatever is nearby. That means that they will start to nip your ears, neck, glasses, jewelry, and possibly eyes. They may not be doing this out of aggression, but it can be anywhere from aggravating to dangerous. The best way to avoid this is not to have your parrot on your shoulder in the first place. Once the bird learns to do this sort of stuff, especially for getting attention, it is very difficult to get it to learn to stop.

To prevent a flying parrot from landing on your shoulder, you can duck or start shaking your shoulder before it lands so that it cannot get on. For a parrot trying to run up your arm, keep your elbow low and bent to make things too steep. Use your other hand to block it from getting to your shoulder.

Now eventually you will want to be able to have your parrot on your shoulder. After all, it keeps your hands free and your parrot happy. The best way to teach good shoulder behavior is to practice it in small doses and with positive outcomes. Put your parrot on your shoulder for just a few seconds but then target it back onto your hand for a treat. If it won't do this, then it isn't good enough at targeting yet and you need to go back to practicing this during training exercises.

Use the single hand target training technique with the clicker, target stick, and treat in one hand to target your parrot from your shoulder onto your hand (figure on page 139, photo on page 295). Put your parrot back on the shoulder and try it again. Repeat about 10 times. You want the parrot to realize that it gets to be on the shoulder in either case, but cooperation gets a treat as well! Letting the parrot back on the shoulder with the treat teaches the parrot that cooperation gets both! To maintain continued cooperation, put the parrot back on your shoulder with treats more often than you put the parrot elsewhere.

Progressively increase the duration your parrot spends on your shoulder prior to taking it back off. Soon, you won't have to use the target stick but just your hand and a treat afterward. Continue to practice dis-shouldering until you can easily take your parrot off. A good strategy for maintaining this down the line is having something good (that isn't a food treat) for your parrot to do as soon as it gets off. It may mean putting it back in the cage for a meal or taking it down to give it head scratches.

The next important thing is to prevent the nippiness. The way to do this is to ensure that your parrot doesn't get bored. To do this, limit duration of shoulder time so that it ends before boredom sets in. Secondly, give your parrot things to watch while it is there. If you can captivate your parrot's attention, it will be too busy to bite. For example, put your parrot on your shoulder when you are doing things such as cleaning, walking around, or making something. Don't put your parrot on your shoulder when you'll be doing something boring (for the parrot). Reading email, watching TV, and other passive activities like this are boring to the bird and it will get agitated and nippy. Don't let it on your shoulder when you expect to do these things to avoid it learning to get nippy.

Shouldering can be used as a reward for a well-behaved parrot. As long as you ensure that coming off the shoulder is equally rewarding as going on, you won't have trouble getting the bird off. Make sure you have a good relationship with the bird before ever allowing it on your shoulder in the first place. Your bird should be at a point that it doesn't bite at all before it goes on your shoulder. Be careful and watch out for displaced aggression and biting (explained in Chapter 8) because you are the closest thing for the bird to bite. Only shoulder your parrot in a safe/stable environment but with enough going on to keep the parrot busy watching. Use shouldering only in moderation and it will be a special reward to your parrot for good behavior.

Potty Training

People fear that keeping parrots flighted will lead them to pooping all over their household, but with a little training and following the potty training procedure, this doesn't have to be the case. Parrots are clean animals and capable of taking their mess elsewhere if given the proper encouragement.

First, you need to understand why parrots may poop everywhere. In the wild, the entire forest is their toilet. The birds live high in the trees and it's not their problem where on the ground their mess ends up. On the other hand, they usually don't poop in their nest or roost because it would directly harm them. Thus, it is important to understand where their natural behavior comes from and learn how to deal with it.

The best approach to potty training involves following a schedule more so than actual training. If you monitor how frequently your parrot poops while it is out (about every 10 minutes for smaller birds and closer to every half hour for larger ones), you will be able to learn the approximate span of time before poops. The simplest and safest approach is to handle your parrot only between this span.

After you have observed your parrot poop, pick up your parrot and handle it as usual. Keep aware of time and be sure to return your parrot several minutes prior to the next expected poop. If you noted that your parrot goes on a regular basis every 15 minutes, then handle your parrot for about 10-12 minutes and set it back on its perch. Ignore the bird and wait until it poops before handling it again. Repeat this process for the rest of your parrot's life and you will rarely, if ever, get pooped on.

The benefit of using this timed approach is that over time it begins to potty train the parrot inadvertently. The parrot will begin to learn that the sooner it goes potty off its perch, the sooner you will pick it up again for continued interaction. Over time, you will be able to handle your bird for differing spans of time and it will learn to either hold it or go early when you set it down.

There is also an additional system for encouraging your parrot to learn to poop when set down on a specific perch. Most parrots actually hold it in overnight and don't poop until they wake up. If you cover your parrot's cage at night, it will ensure that the parrot remains asleep until you take it out. Uncover the cage and make haste to pick up your bird and take it to its potty perch. At first, I would suggest setting the potty perch just outside the cage for quick transfer. Over time, the bird will learn to hold it till set down there.

Eventually, you will learn your parrot's body language prior to pooping and will know when one is imminent. When you set the bird down on a perch and expect it to go, say "poop" or "go potty" or even "bomb's away" if you wish. Stay consistent with your cue and say it every time before the bird poops. Eventually, even if the bird wasn't going to, you may be able to invoke it to go preemptively by using the cue.

Now what exactly is a potty perch? Quite simply, it's any perch that you want your parrot to take care of business from. You should have a clear area below to place a newspaper to make cleaning easy. You have the option of either teaching the bird to use a specific potty perch or just any place you set your parrot down on. Since your parrot learns to poop as soon as possible after being set down on a perch, this also helps to keep it from pooping on the fly. Your bird will develop a habit of pooping upon landing instead. So if you are sitting with your bird and potty time is coming up, all you have to do is send your bird to fly back to its perch to poop. Wait until it poops and then recall it to fly back to you. With a clipped parrot you would have to get up every time to set the bird down and if you managed to forget, the bird will have an accident on you. But, a flighted parrot has the option to bail to its perch when it needs to go or you can send it back. It is actually the well-trained flying parrot that has the advantage for potty training and not the clipped one.

A byproduct of the healthy feeding schedule (which was mentioned in Chapter 4) is that the bird will be more empty during the times you are handling it and thus poop less frequently. Since following the complete approach of this book will have you mainly take your parrot out only prior to scheduled meal times, the parrot will be at its emptiest during handling. We don't schedule feeding with this purpose, but since it is already being done for health reasons, you benefit from the parrot pooping less while out of the cage.

One thing to avoid is engaging in any sort of formal training for the purpose of potty training. Do not use the clicker, treats, or any substantial rewards. It has been said that this makes parrots hold it in too long and can lead to health issues. The goal is to learn the timing, follow a schedule, and to encourage the parrot to potty in specific places only. This does 95% of the job and for the other 5%, just learn to live with it because accidents will still occasionally happen.

Carrier

You will have to take your parrot out of the house at least at some point in its life. If you follow the recommendations in this book, it will actually occur quite frequently (parrots need to go outdoors for training reasons as much as for health). Besides the desirability of teaching your parrot to go in a carrier so you could take it on outings, the bird will occasionally need to visit a veterinarian, groomer, or someone to board it. Installing a perch makes any carrier a lot more suitable for parrots. You can use either a carrier or a travel cage depending on availability and the size of your bird.

For very young baby birds, you will most likely be able to just get away with sticking the bird in the carrier and going places. The carrier is nest-like and baby birds just go along with what their parents tell them, so this is all you would need to do. If you continue regularly taking your parrot on outings this way from when it is a baby, you shouldn't need to train it to go in or out of the carrier. Chapter 9 will teach you how to make parrot outings reinforcing enough for your parrot to go in/out of the carrier voluntarily.

If you acquired a rehomed parrot or have owned yours for some time, carrier training will be necessary. And even if you have a baby or your older bird already goes in a carrier, it cannot hurt to go through these steps to improve the process even further. If your parrot has ever been abused in the past to the point that it fears carriers, you will need to begin by desensitizing it to carriers from scratch. Chapter 9 describes how to introduce scary objects so refer to that and apply it to the carrier to get started, if your bird will absolutely go nowhere near it.

Once you are able to get your parrot in the vicinity of the carrier without it freaking out, you can turn this into a training exercise. Do this during normal training time to have peak motivation and do not expect to do this five minutes before needing to put your parrot in the carrier. Carrier training must be done beforehand in an unrushed setting. Place the carrier on a table or on the floor. Put the parrot down away from the carrier and begin targeting. At first don't target the bird toward the carrier at all. Target your parrot to random places so it can learn to ignore the carrier and focus on the exercise. As the parrot gets better, begin to progressively target it closer and closer to the carrier. You can double your improvement by targeting the bird toward the carrier some and then offering the treat closer to the carrier so that it has to take a few more steps closer to gets its reward. When you can get your parrot to target all the way up to the carrier, don't immediately target it inside. Instead, target the parrot around all sides of the carrier and onto the top of it. If it can't easily climb/fly up to the top, you can place it on top to target it around.

When your parrot is fully comfortable around the outside of the carrier, you will be able to use the target method to target it into the carrier. You can put the target stick in through an air hole so that the parrot can only get to the stick by going inside. At first only target the parrot to step a little into the carrier and offer treats outside, but eventually work it deeper inside. Do not close the door or force the parrot to stay in the carrier though. You never want the bird to have a bad experience on the first day with anything new. On a follow up session, quickly repeat the above steps and begin to close the door on the carrier when the parrot is inside. Drop treats into the carrier to keep the bird busy and then open the door to let it back out.

After the parrot can go in/out of the carrier on its own, the rest of the training is easy but is long term. To get the bird from just going into the carrier to being comfortable staying in it for spans of time, begin to feed your parrot its scheduled meals in the carrier. After training, instead of putting the parrot back into the cage, some days put it into the carrier along with its meal instead. The first few times you do this, let the bird out after it completes its meal. But later on, leave the bird in for half an hour, two hours, even a day at a time. Provide, water, toys, perches, and things for it to do while inside, but eventually it will learn to just chill in the carrier.

The results of this training will be most helpful if you ever need to travel with your bird for up to a few days at a time. Once you reach the point when you can let the parrot spend prolonged periods in the carrier, leave the carrier unattended in random rooms of your house. This simulates visiting a new location. Just be sure that other people or pets cannot pose a danger to the parrot in the unattended carrier. After this point, you will easily be able to take your parrot out for grooming or on outings without fear that the carrier will cause any harm to your relationship. In fact, your parrot will by then be so accustomed to the carrier that it will bring it comfort and safety in unfamiliar places.

Grooming

Parrots' claws can grow to be very sharp so occasional grooming will become necessary. The purpose of this guide is not to teach you how to perform the actual procedure (it can result in bleeding or injury if done incorrectly so please have a professional perform it or learn about it from other reliable sources) but how to make it as worry-free for your parrot as possible.

There is a common misconception that owners should not trim their parrot's talons because then their parrot will hate them. The simple fact is that **no one should ever do anything to your parrot** (except perhaps for emergency medical care where there may be no other choice) **that could cause it to hate anyone**! I cannot stress this point enough. If anyone, even someone other than you, is known by the parrot to do devastating things to it, it will cause your parrot to distrust humans in general. This is exactly the opposite of the well-behaved parrot relationship that you are seeking to establish. The goal is to have your parrot hate no one (because as you will see in later chapters, hating some people can cause the parrot to bite other people!). This means that your parrot must tolerate or better yet enjoy the grooming process.

Let's face it, there is nothing enjoyable about getting something trimmed. But it's not too terrible either. The worst part of grooming is the tight grabbing, forcefulness, abruptness, insecurity, helplessness, and the feeling of no way out. These elements are actually the greater reason most parrots fear grooming rather than the actual painless snap on their claws.

Now the grab/toweling skills of Chapter 3 actually come into practical use. If the parrot never had a reason to fear being grabbed or toweled, that aspect will already be less detrimental. If your parrot has already been accustomed to regular handling, touching, toweling, and grabbing in a good context, then the bird won't fear these things during grooming. This is why I prefer to groom my own birds and would encourage you to learn how to as well. However, since it's a good idea to watch someone else do it at least once, so you can learn, I am going to provide advice how to make the grooming go better when someone else does it.

Since your parrot is already on a healthy feeding plan, treats are a big deal any time of day. Bring your bird's favorite treats along for the grooming. Don't go straight to grooming when you arrive at the location. Instead, take your bird out for a little while and have it stay on your hand. Possibly, even do some targeting or tricks to distract it from the new environment. Don't allow the groomer to grab the bird out of the carrier or do things their way. They don't realize or care about the fact that there are psychological repercussions to their approach that parrot owners will later have to face. Instead, follow your normal grab training routine to get your parrot to volunteer for you to grab it for treats. You will be the one holding the parrot and not the groomer. You will also be the source of treats for cooperation.

Use your grab to hold the bird with feet toward the groomer and allow the groomer to trim one talon. Release the bird and give it a treat. You can cup the parrot against your body for comfort, reassurance, and to prevent it from flying off. Continue this process but progressively do a few more talons at a time. You may or may not choose to use a towel depending on how the parrot is handling the whole thing. I think it is better to do the grooming without a towel if your parrot is already accustomed to being grabbed.

Once you have learned sufficiently about how to trim the talons yourself, it can benefit you and your parrot (bearing in mind that if done incorrectly, it can cause your parrot to bleed profusely). You can make it even less uncomfortable for your parrot by trimming only a single talon per session. Your parrot will have very little to fear or hate you for, when all it has to do is be grabbed, get one little snip, and then receive a jackpot of treats in return.

Your parrot's beak should not have to be trimmed. If the beak is overgrown, this is a possible sign of improper nutrition or disease. However, it is sometimes desirable to perform a shallow cosmetic trim. Do not cut the beak with any form of cutter. Only run a coarse nail file across the under tip of the beak a few times to blunt the tip.

You can use positive reinforcement to train your parrot to voluntarily give you its foot for nail grooming (photo on page 296). It is easiest and safest to do this type of trim with a nail trimmer stone or a file. You can order a Parrot Nail Trimmer Stone and see my detailed free video on how to train a parrot for voluntary nail trimming at www.ParrotWizard.com/Nail_Trimmer.

The reason there is no mention of techniques for wing clipping is because this book does not advocate the process. Wing clipping should neither be necessary for good parrot behavior, nor does it lead to it. Therefore, wing trimming is not recommended.

Out of Cage Time

Parrots are highly intelligent and exceptionally social creatures. They don't just enjoy attention, they need it for their psychological well-being. Often, you will read or hear about the number of hours a certain species requires to spend outside of the cage. In reality, there is no defined amount. There is no saying that a cockatoo requires a minimum of 3 hours outside the cage while a cockatiel requires 30 minutes. It comes down to quality over quantity and habit over numbers.

Keeping a clipped parrot on a tree or play stand while you go about your daily business is hardly better than keeping it in a cage. The bird is still constrained to a single location and deprived of free will. Furthermore, keeping a parrot out but ignored may encourage bad behaviors such as screaming or biting for attention. Focusing on spending quality time together will go a longer way to enhance your relationship than focusing on duration.

Find activities that you can involve your parrot in. Take your parrot out when you are sorting laundry or doing something active. Avoid having the parrot out when you are doing something passive (such as reading or watching TV) because the parrot will get bored and lean toward undesirable attention seeking behavior. Likewise, avoid having your bird out when you are stressed or doing something important. Have your parrot out whenever you know you will be able to provide attention or at least something for the parrot to watch you do.

Flighted time outside the cage is also very valuable because the parrot can exercise and explore. However, this sort of time out must be supervised because of household hazards. Outdoor and travel time is also an excellent activity for your parrot. Whenever you are walking or driving somewhere, you can bring your parrot with you. Grab a harness and take your parrot along. Remember that out of cage time isn't merely about the parrot spending time out of the cage, but about having an enriched interactive experience. Spending time with pets is fun, so enjoy it!

Chapter 5 Checklist:

☐ Good behavior needs to be taught, practiced, and maintained
☐ Have the parrot step up to come out of the cage
☐ Do not force the parrot out of the cage
☐ Give the parrot the chance to come to a perch by the door
☐ Do not feed the parrot outside the cage except for training
☐ Put the parrot back into the cage for meals
☐ Weigh your parrot consistently every morning
☐ Monitor weight for unexpected weight loss or changes
☐ Train petting etiquette until the parrot enjoys petting
☐ Keep the parrot off your shoulder until it's trained
☐ Use target training to target the parrot off your shoulder
☐ Return the parrot to shoulder with a treat most of the time
☐ Make sure the place parrot goes after shoulder is rewarding
☐ Avoid the parrot getting bored while on your shoulder
☐ Learn your parrot's poop schedule and predict next time
☐ Set your parrot down until it poops before resuming activity
☐ Use target training to get your parrot used to travel carrier
☐ Practice taming exercises in preparation for grooming
☐ Provide quality out of cage time daily

Chapter 6: Flight

Flight is one of the most unique aspects of owning a bird and also one of the most rewarding. People should stop seeing flight as an undesirable trait that must be clipped away. Instead, I hope you can realize what an integral part of the parrot's parrotness flight really is! Breeders, bird stores, groomers, and other owners of clipped parrots will downplay the importance of flight or even go so far as to scare you into preventing it. What they don't realize is that not allowing a parrot to fly actually creates more behavioral problems than it solves!

Birds require flight as much as ground animals require the ability to walk. Their entire body is evolved for flight. The perfect balance of strength and lightness is present as in no other animal. Obviously, their wings are evolved for flight. But, what may be less obvious is that so are all of the parrot's internal organs. The cardiovascular system is evolved to rapidly deliver blood to flight muscles and the brain at over 300 beats per minute in flight. The body temperature is at a perpetual fever to allow for the quickest processing of food into energy. The respiratory system allows the bird to take bigger breaths of air and deliver oxygen quicker to the flight muscles. The crop, gizzard, and digestive system are optimized for storing food and providing energy on the go. All of these systems are not simply capable of flight, they require it. Without flight, these organs cannot develop or be maintained properly for the body which the bird possesses.

Biting, screaming, and feather plucking are all side effects of clipping. I do not know of a solution to these problems (or their prevention) that does not include flight. Obesity, boredom, excessive energy, and many other issues are also the result of making a captive bird idle and flightless.

Perhaps it is not flight but idleness that causes problems, but there is nothing as physically and mentally demanding for a bird as flight.

I realize that keeping parrots flighted has become the subject of much controversy, but it really shouldn't be. Birds are born with wings – this should come as no surprise. Up until recently, people were unaware of ways to share a home with flighted parrots. Clipping seemed like the only way. This practice is particularly the byproduct of the wild-caught parrot trade. Those wild parrots did not know how to fly in a home and wanted nothing to do with humans. Now with hand-raised, domestically bred parrots, these reasons are no longer valid. Furthermore, with the all-encompassing approach that you are learning (such as how to get the parrot to step up willingly, how to put the parrot away, how to make it not fear you grabbing it, etc) having an out of control bird freely roaming your home should no longer be a concern. By using this approach you will gain your parrot's trust and if anything you'll have a harder time keeping it off of you than on!

Flight Safety

Safety is most often cited as the reason to clip parrots. However, these safety concerns usually have nothing to do with the parrot being flighted and everything to do with the owner taking some responsibility. Excuses like "flighted parrots fall into toilets, pots of boiling water, and other dangerous places" have more to do with the owner keeping the parrot out during unsafe activity than whether or not it can fly. A clipped parrot can just as well fall off the owner's shoulder into a pot of boiling water. The safe approach is not to have parrots out during cooking, keep bathroom doors closed, don't leave unsafe objects out and don't clip the parrot.

Other reasons for clipping include: keeping the parrot from flying out of doors/windows, keeping the parrot from flying off when outside, other pets, and "attitude adjustment." Although these are potential hazards, they actually exist for clipped parrots as well, and it is important to provide safeguards in either case. A clipped bird can often fly just enough that it might make it out a window and out of sight. The proper precaution is to keep the window closed rather than take a chance. When it comes to doors, it is important to always have a second door to prevent a direct path to outside. As for taking the parrot outdoors, a gust of wind or other natural air force can actually be enough to carry a parrot into the air and quite far away. Clipped parrots usually panic and don't know what to do when it comes to flight, so this is a risky practice. Instead, it is safer to take any parrot outside in a carrier or wearing a flight harness. Later in this chapter you will learn about the use of a harness as a more reliable failsafe for taking parrots outdoors compared to clipping. Finally, when it comes to this concept of clipping a parrot's wings for an "attitude adjustment," it is simply dreadful. If the owner would take the time to realize why the parrot behaves the way it does, they would be able to solve the problem rather than just mask it by clipping. With clipping, the issue never gets resolved, it just leaves the parrot powerless to act on it. This is neither a loving approach nor does it lead to a well-behaved parrot. Allowing a parrot the freedom to fly, and then setting things up so that it wants to fly to you anyway, is the ultimate mark of a well-behaved parrot.

Teaching a Parrot to Fly

If your parrot is already clipped but is transitioning to flight – or even if your parrot is a baby that wasn't clipped, but not yet a good flier – there will be a tough transitional stage to get through while the parrot learns to fly. Believe it or not, birds are not born knowing how to fly. Like toddlers discover their legs, birds have to discover how to use their wings. Like the toddler learning to walk, there will be some falls and miscalculations along the way. This is one of the strongest reasons for not clipping young birds; their bones are still soft and they don't get very seriously injured if/when they crash into things. It's tougher for an older bird to learn to fly but with the right guidance, there is no reason it can't be done.

Often when a previously clipped bird starts to fly again, owners watch it crash into things and use this as a justification to clip again. They don't realize the main reason why this is happening though. It's not because parrots can't learn to fly indoors, it's just that the parrot never has. Add to that the fact that not all of its flight feathers have grown in and its wing muscles have atrophied and are weak, so the bird just isn't ready to be an ace flier. Given time, however, the bird can learn to fly even in adulthood.

Some things to do to help protect a learning bird at first include covering windows with blinds, letting it fly in smaller spaces where it can't get as much speed, and using a controlled methodology. The ideal time to begin this process is just as the parrot begins growing back its flight feathers, or with a baby, as soon as possible. Don't throw a parrot to encourage it to fly and don't wait to begin the training until your parrot is flying and crashing into things on its own. Once 2-4 primary flight feathers have grown back in, the clipped parrot will have sufficient capability to start this process. You will help rehabilitate the bird's flight muscles as you follow this procedure and in return the parrot will learn the loyalty of flying to you.

A gentle way to teach a parrot to fly is to use two perches and targeting. I personally designed the Parrot Training Perch kit for doing this and provide it for sale at http://TrainingPerch.com. However, you can use two chair backs as a free alternative. These are less ideal because chairs aren't always the right height or size but they can make do. The way to begin this training is to start with your two perches parallel to each other and within walking distance for the parrot.

To start the flight training, use the targeting method (target, clicker, treat as described in Chapter 4) to encourage the parrot to walk back and forth between the parallel perches. Spread the gap between the perches with successive attempts (refer to figure on page 157 and photos on page 300). Ideally the process should be done slowly enough so that the bird will seamlessly learn to hop from perch to perch and eventually fly. More realistically, you may reach a gap too long for the parrot to walk/climb across that it will refuse to come. Just bring the perches back closer together and keep practicing. At some point, you will sneak in a gap just big enough that out of habit the parrot will still try to step across but in reality won't be able to make it across the gap without flying. As the bird begins to fall, it will reflexively throw its wings out and end up making its first flight. After a few times, it will realize what those flapper things on its arms are for and will make flapping hops to cross the gap between the perches. Once this vital realization has been made, progress will only be limited by the parrot's physical capability and endurance. During successive sessions, continue widening the gap but never more than what the parrot can do. Soon, you can eliminate the target stick and merely point at the perch while saying something like "come." Since all the parrot has been doing the last bunch of times is hopping from perch to perch, it will continue to do this and learn the new cue without the aid of a target stick.

Within a few successful training sessions, you will want to begin *recall training*. Having the parrot fly from perch to perch may be great exercise, but you may as well have the parrot learn to fly to you! Place your hand (or entire arm) in front of the second perch that you've been targeting your bird to. Target or point to your hand (the same way as to the perch) and encourage your parrot to do the same as before. But now, the parrot should fly to your hand instead. Start at close range. Slowly increase the distance like you did for perch to perch flights. This is the beginning of flight recall training!

You can begin to phase out saying "come" or pointing and just call your parrot's name instead. The reason I suggest calling your parrot by name rather than saying "fly to me" or any other generic phrase is because if you ever have another bird, they may get confused as to which one you call; but if you always call your birds by name, then only the one called will come to you.

I recommend using your outstretched hand (out to your side) as the recall command. Not only does it provide a lot of room for your parrot to land, it is also a distinct visible sign that the parrot can see from afar. If your parrot is ever stuck up a tree, it will easily recognize the outstretched arm as a cue to flight recall. You will also notice that *step up* uses the back of the hand whereas flight recall uses the front (fingerprint side). This helps differentiate your intentions to the parrot while in close proximity. This tells the bird whether to wait for you to come close enough so it can step up or to fly to you now.

You will also want to work on an equally important flight skill: returning to the perch. While still practicing short distance flight recalls, it is your best opportunity to target your parrot to fly from your hand back to its perch. Point the target stick to the perch to train your parrot to fly there. When it lands, click and provide a treat. When the parrot finishes eating, recall it to your hand for a treat. Let it eat on your hand and target it back to the perch. Use a command such as "go to perch" every time you target your parrot to fly from your hand to its perch. After a little practice, you will no longer need to use the target stick and will simply be able to use the command. This will free your limitation from arm-span-range flights to longer ones. You will be able to recall the parrot farther and farther and then say "go to perch." Watch the bird fly back, click when it lands, and then walk over to give it a treat.

Continue sending your parrot places by pointing to a perch and then having your parrot fly there for a reward. You will be teaching the bird which places you would prefer it fly to and spend time on. Point to the parrot's cage, tree, training perch, or other location to signal the bird to fly there. This skill will be very important when using long flights for exercise so that the bird can be flown back and forth. You will be able to phase out giving treats for going back to the perch, so rest assured you won't have to run long distances after your bird just to give treats. Simply recall the parrot, give it a reward, point to its perch, and say "go to perch". If it doesn't go on its own, move your arm forward quickly so that it has to fly. Since you are not providing a stable platform for it to eat on, it has to fly back to its perch to consume the treat. Furthermore, returning to the training perch sets it up for another recall opportunity and more treats. So after the initial learning stage you won't really have to reward "return to perch" flights.

Continue practicing a variety of flight skills with your parrot until it's an ace and will fly to you from anywhere. Progressively increase distances, recall around obstacles, and keep challenging the bird. Recall from low to high and from high to low. Recall the parrot from the floor up to your hand. Recall your parrot down a staircase. The down flight is actually an important one to practice, as it provides a means of recovering your parrot from a tree if it were ever to get outside. Also practice out of sight recalls where your parrot cannot see you when you call it. This by-voice out-of-sight recall is also a great skill for bird recovery.

Not only will you find flight training beneficial but also a lot of fun. It's exciting to watch your parrot zoom around your home with skill and ease and come to you when you call.

One problem you may encounter is that your parrot will be very eager to fly to you when food rewards are given but not between training. One remedy is to deformalize the flight training by recalling at random times and then giving it very desirable treats. Another way is to simply accept that your parrot is an active flier during training and not at other times. Within the confines of your home, it's not really a big deal if your parrot doesn't fly to you on command at any hour of the day. You can always revert to having it step up. This is an easier strategy that still ensures that your parrot becomes a skilled flier, gets sufficient exercise, and can eventually be recovered if lost. Since the parrot will be used to flying to you when it is hungry, it will eventually get hungry enough that your recall will work. It is up to you to what extent you wish to master flight recall, but as long as the basics are established, safety is well assured.

Fun With Flight

There are many thrilling flight-related activities that you can pursue with your parrot. You can play hide-and-seek with your parrot, teach it to fly through hoops, play flighted fetch, and teach all of your parrots to flock fly to you at once.

The reason this chapter about flight comes before the chapter about trick training is because the parrot needs to be eager to fly to you before you can get your hands on the bird to teach the tricks. Therefore, I suggest teaching target first, then flight recall, then regular non-flighted tricks. After you've had success with those steps, come back to this section to learn about teaching tricks that involve flight.

Hide-and-seek is the easiest flight game that you can involve your parrot in since it is nothing more than an extension of the flight recall skills learned previously. The key is to transition from visible recall to non-visible recall. This could mean peeking around a doorway and practicing recalls prior to fully hiding out of sight. Transition slowly by moving more and more out of the bird's sight. In the last stage you'll peek out, call your bird, and as it is coming, retreat to your hiding place. The bird will still remember where you just were and come. Eventually, it will be able to locate you merely by the sound of your voice.

To teach your parrot to fly through hoops, have it fly many flight recalls in the presence of a vertical hoop. Either have someone hold the hoop or buy a hoop stand. Call your parrot from a training perch in close proximity to the hoop so that the only way to reach you is through the hoop. Once the bird learns to fly through the hoop, increase the distance. Move slightly to the side of the hoop. Now, the bird will have to choose between flying straight to you or divert to go through the hoop. If it goes through the hoop, reward. If it doesn't, then don't. Eventually, it will catch on that in sight of the hoop it must go through before coming to you.

If you've taught your parrot the hoop flight trick, you can use that skill to teach boomerang flight (where the parrot flies away from you, turns around and comes back to you). Set the hoop away from you, send the bird to fly through it. The bird will return to you after flying through the hoop to receive a treat. Every time you do this, say a command such as "boomerang" or "go fly." Eventually, you will be able to remove the hoop but still use the command to tell the bird to fly where the hoop used to be and then come back. Keep practicing this maneuver in alternate locations until the command is known.

An alternative way to teach boomerang flight without the requisite hoop trick is to send the bird off in flight (either by swinging your arm forward or tossing it) and as it's flying, doing a flight recall by calling its name. This is a more difficult way to teach the trick because not only does it require maximum motivation but also outstanding flight skills. Thus, I cannot recommend this method for most owners, but since it was successful for me, I am presenting it here.

Find a treat that your parrot goes crazy for. Let it see it in your hand but toss the bird away. The bird may come back on its own or you may recall it. If it turns around and comes back to you, click and reward. Put it on cue by saying "boomerang" or whatever you want to call it as you toss the bird. Boomerang flight is more than just a silly trick, it's actually a great skill to teach your parrot since it encourages your parrot to return to you. So if your parrot were to fly off outside (on a harness) or in a large indoor public place, it would be accustomed to returning to you when frightened.

Flighted fetch can be taught to a parrot that already knows the fetch trick (Chapter 7) and flight recall. It's simply a matter of putting the two together. If your bird is already an outstanding flier, it may well make the connection on its own. Put an object on the floor for it to retrieve and place the bird on the floor near it. Have it fetch the object to your hand a few times. Then kneel and hold your hand high enough so that the bird cannot simply step on it. Put one hand out for recall and the other hand (the one the bird will place the fetched object into) near it. Eager to get the treat by retrieving the object for you, the parrot will fly up to your hand and finish the trick. You can provide some extra encouragement by recalling your parrot as it picks up the object. After a bit more practice, you will be able to stand upright with the parrot on your shoulder, toss an object on the ground, and the bird will fly down, retrieve it, and then fly back up to your shoulder. The bird will hold the object until you bring your hand up for the bird to hand it over to you.

If your parrot isn't a very good flier, consistently drops the object, or doesn't fly with it, you can teach it to fly with something in its beak using the following method. Place two chairs up against each other (or coffee tables or other flat surfaces that can line up). Place the object on one chair and your hand on the other. Have the parrot walk from chair to chair to bring the object to you. Slowly start spreading the gap between chairs with successive attempts so that the parrot hops over and eventually has to fly over the gap. Practice this some more and then get rid of the second chair. Have the parrot fly to land on one of your hands while it deposits the object into the other.

The last nifty flight trick I will discuss is flock recall. This is when two or more parrots fly to you simultaneously to recall. Under normal recall training, the goal is to have only the named parrot fly to you when called and not the others. But for this one and only time, they are all to fly together. This trick requires heightened motivation, so the best reward will be going back into the cage to receive a meal. If you set up the feeding schedule the way this book recommends, all of your parrots should already know when you're about to put them away and eagerly await this opportunity. To differentiate the visual cue from a single recall, stretch out both arms parallel to the ground (forming a T). This provides maximum separation between birds and maximum surface for them to land on if there are many. The trick to getting all the birds to come at once is to use a unified command (such as "come birds" or "everyone come") and then call them individually. This way they will eventually learn to come as a group when seeing that cue and hearing the call. The harder part is to get the birds to learn what spot to land on and not get discouraged by having no place to go. To solve this, you can start with this training in short range. Put every bird on its own training perch next to each other and call them with your arms out. If you have more than two birds, you can try to simplify the situation by teaching two at a time and then adding on others later.

Harness Training

Even though harness training does not involve flight directly, it is very relevant to managing a parrot outdoors safely. A harness can be used both to allow a parrot to fly outside and to prevent it from flying off unexpectedly.

Consider a harness to be like a seatbelt in a car. A seatbelt is not something that keeps you safe day to day; careful driving does! But, it is there to protect you in an accident when you least expect it! Thus, you use it all the time. Likewise, a harness should not be the primary means of preventing a parrot from flying off. Your relationship, training, and approach, like careful driving, should be the reason your parrot does not fly away from you outdoors. The harness is not a chain to hold the bird down, but rather a safety net to catch it in the unlikely event of a spook. These events should be rare but a harness can be a lifesaver when they do occur.

This harness discussion is as important for clipped parrots as it is for flighted ones when it comes to going outside. Even clipped parrots could potentially fly off outdoors, so it is best to use a harness for them as well as for flighted parrots. A clipped parrot can fly just far enough to end up landing on the street. A harness will ensure any parrot stays close to you when out in public or near traffic.

Unlike a travel carrier, a harness can provide a more interactive outdoor experience for you and your parrot. With larger parrots it may be the only practical way to safely take them outside. Direct natural sunlight is essential for parrot health and flying outdoors can provide great exercise.

Teaching a parrot to wear a harness is one of the most challenging training exercises because a high level of taming as well as training is required. Parrots are not familiar with ever wearing anything on their body. Asking a parrot to wear a harness is quite unusual, so a lot of training and practice is necessary. Although baby parrots may simply allow you to stick a harness on them without much fuss, adults are likely to be resistant. Training will ensure that the parrot not only agrees to wear a harness, but is actually happy to do so.

While it is important to select a quality harness that is suitably sized for your parrot, no harness will convince a parrot to just wear it. The training effort you put into harness training will play a far greater role on your harness success than which harness or color you choose. I have been using and recommending the Aviator Harness for over ten years.

You must have a very close, hands-on relationship with your parrot before even thinking of using a harness. Hopefully the information presented throughout this book will encourage you and help you achieve these requisites as you go along. The next critical thing to remember is not to take your parrot's tameness for granted and just stick the harness on. This is a likely way to ruin the good relationship you already established. Even if you could get away with putting the harness on by holding the bird down or tricking it, the bird will be quick to remember the unpleasant experience and flee the harness (or worse yet, you) in the future. Instead, follow the training tips outlined below (unless the bird is a very young hand tame baby, then you can get away with just putting the harness on – but when it grows older you will likely need to return to follow these steps anyway).

Always attach the leash end of the harness to your belt or belt loop. Never use the leash on your wrist. Not only is it risky but also distracting. If your parrot flies off (whether home or outside) and the leash slips off, the parrot is liable to get caught on things and get hurt. You can purchase a key chain carabiner hook to quickly and securely clip the leash to your belt. From that point forward you don't have to think about it until you remove the harness. This also allows you to take multiple birds out with you. Always clip the leash onto your belt even before you approach the bird with the harness (photo on page 302).

The most important part of harness training does not even involve the harness itself! Put away and do not attempt to use the harness until the requisite taming and training are complete. Follow the steps in Chapter 4 to establish a training routine, motivation, target training, and hand taming. A parrot that is unfamiliar with training or is not comfortable being touched by hands will be especially uncomfortable with a harness.

The harness training outlined here is based on using an Aviator Harness, however with some modification can be used with any bird harness.

The first step of harness training consists of hand taming exercises. The goal is to be able to hold your hand near, above, and on the bird without it moving or reacting. Review the hand taming process to get started. Then repeat the hand taming exercise, like you did on the parrot's head, but from the side to approach the wings. Hover the hand from the side facing the wing. Continue closer and closer until you can touch the wing. Reward each time the bird stays still. Begin putting a finger underneath the wing and with successive attempts start to open the wing a little. You will likely find that the parrot resists and tries to pull the wing shut. Continue practicing until the parrot learns to hold the wing loose and allows you to open it. In addition to touching the head, you will have to be able to handle the wings in order to maneuver them into the harness. Don't forget to repeat the exercise for the other wing as well.

Now you are ready to introduce the harness. The first step is to get your parrot accustomed to the harness material. If the bird has never had a bad experience with the harness, this should be fairly simple. If your parrot is terrified of the harness, greater care will need to be put into this process. Drape the harness around your shoulders so that your hands are free while you wear it. Prepare a clicker, target stick, and a treat. Slowly approach the parrot while turning your body so that the harness is not even visible to the bird. Begin a routine of target training the parrot. Little by little, turn your body to expose more of the harness to the bird. The bird will begin to see the harness while still being engaged in the targeting exercise. Once you are able to move in close and let the bird see the harness, you can begin touching the harness with your free hand. This will help the bird realize that even if you are handling the harness, you won't be forcing it onto the bird.

Repeat the hand taming exercise over the parrot's head (described in Chapter 4), but this time with the harness. Hide most of the harness in your fist, exposing only a small piece. Hover your hand with the harness from far away and give a treat. Move in closer and closer and give treats each time. Start showing bigger and bigger amounts of the harness. Just outside of bite range, work on improving duration by giving multiple treats in a row. Improve patience by giving multiple treats in slow motion. Continue getting closer and closer with the harness until you can touch the parrot's head with the harness. Proceed to repeating the grab training but with the harness between the bird and your hand to simulate wearing the harness without actually wearing it.

Once you are certain that your parrot not only has no fear of the harness but may even like it, begin the actual harness training. The secret to harness training is not to put the harness on the parrot but to train the parrot to put the harness on itself. After all, if the parrot chooses to wear it, then it will not be upset with you or the harness and actually get to enjoy being outside.

The collar for the harness is usually pretty tight so it makes it difficult to train a parrot to start wearing it. Wouldn't it be great if you had a bigger collar to practice with? No worries, you won't have to run out and buy a bigger size harness. You actually already have one in the properly sized harness you already bought! You can slide the collar out of the way and use the strap of the harness in a circle to make a much larger training collar.

With your parrot on a training perch, show the loop of the fake collar and stick your target stick through the collar. This way the parrot does not even have to reach through the collar, your outreached hand is doing all the work. But, little by little, with subsequent targets, target your parrot closer and closer to the held collar. Eventually, the parrot will be abeam the collar and soon even reaching into it. Target through the collar and give treats through the collar to improve duration (figure on page 171, photo on page 302). Keep practicing targeting your parrot to stick its head deeper and deeper through the artificial collar. Once this is successful, continue to practice this but make the collar smaller and smaller as you progress. Eventually, the fake collar will be the same size as the real collar. Don't stop here. Keep practicing with the training collar becoming smaller than the real one. This is a chance to over-practice so that the real collar will seem easy by comparison. The difference is that if the parrot suddenly wants to get out, with the fake collar, all you have to do is release the collar and it will get big and the parrot can get out. Not so easy with the real one.

It is very important that you don't approach the parrot with the collar, but instead have the parrot walk to the collar by itself. Always hold the collar at a distance from the parrot and draw the parrot toward the collar using the target stick. The goal is not just to get the collar onto the parrot but to get the parrot to choose to wear it.

Repeat the exercise with the parrot targeting into the real collar (photo on page 303). Phase out the target stick by making it shorter and shorter. Hold the target stick lower with the rest hidden in your hand. Also hold the target stick too far away now so that the parrot never even reaches it. Just click the clicker when the parrot inserts its head into the collar. Now you will no longer need the target stick. Just show the collar to the parrot from the side of the training perch and have the parrot walk over and stick its head into the collar by itself.

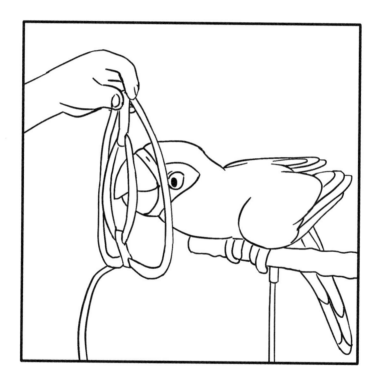

The last stage involves putting on the wing straps (and/or buckles). Be sure to practice donning the harness on a stuffed animal or in the air so that you are familiar with the process before actually performing it on the bird. Teaching the parrot to wear the complete harness involves taking one step forward and then taking the full harness back off. Put the harness on a little further with each successive try, but always remove the harness before going far. The smaller the steps, the easier it will go. The parrot needs practice taking the harness off as much as putting it on. Feed treats continuously during this process. This is partly to make the parrot feel highly rewarded, but it also serves to keep the beak full and out of the way. Whenever you remove the harness, always have the parrot walk over to put the collar on before practicing putting more of the harness on the next time.

First, put part of one wing in and take it back off. Next time, put a little more wing in. Continue making progress for a little more of the complete harness coming on, but always take it back off. This helps the parrot build stamina for wearing the harness and not feel trapped. Feed treats one after another the entire time the harness is coming on as well as off.

Eventually, you will be able to put on the complete harness. Do not immediately take advantage of this and go outside. Remove it and practice some more. Have the parrot eat a large treat such as a nut or even an entire meal while wearing the harness at home. Always remove the harness when the bird is finished eating and before it can get bored. Bored parrots tend to chew on the harness and then they are learning the wrong behavior. Prevent the parrot from learning to chew the harness by always having the parrot occupied while wearing it. To wrap up the harness training and for practical day to day use, give the parrot a huge treat such as a nut in shell for voluntarily putting the collar on. The bird will not have the opportunity to eat this while you continue putting the harness on. The nut will keep the beak full and away from interfering while you put the rest of the harness on. The nut will serve as a reward for voluntarily putting the collar on and for waiting for you to finish putting on the entire harness. Once the parrot is done with the nut, either remove the harness or immediately head outside. Being outside is distracting enough for the parrot to be busy looking around rather than chewing on the harness.

If your parrot has not been outside before, it's a good idea to take it out a few times in a carrier to get more used to being outdoors prior to doing this wearing a harness. The best mindset for using a harness is to treat it as though it isn't there and think of it as nothing more than a backup. This means when you take your parrot out wearing it the first few times, be careful that the bird does not fly off. This is important. If the bird has a bad experience wearing the harness, it will be much more reluctant to let you put it on again. Thus for your first few outings, start by cupping the bird against your body, then work toward allowing it to perch on your hand but hold its feet, then let it perch freely while you still grip the leash close so that it is impossible for the parrot to fly off your hand. Only after multiple successful sessions like this, should you let the parrot perch freely on your hand, shoulder, or a perch. After this point, if the bird flies off and crashes, it will learn not to fly off rather than to hate the harness entirely.

Since your parrot has already learned indoor flight recall as a prerequisite, teaching outdoor harness flight recall should not be too much of a challenge. It may require greater food motivation to overcome the novelty of being outdoors. However, following the recall methodology over again while outside should quickly remind the parrot what to do. Bring a target stick and use it to target the parrot to fly onto your hand outside.

By following this method, the parrot will learn not to fly much while wearing the harness unless called. This is best.

Avoid free flying the parrot while it is wearing a harness (where it can fly wherever it wants within the radius of its leash). Instead, keep the parrot grounded while on the short leash or let it only fly moderated flight recall when on a leash extension. This way the parrot can still enjoy outdoor sunshine and remain free flighted indoors. It is a reasonable compromise for the parrot to be able to go outdoors and free fly only indoors, just not at the same time.

With a harness trained parrot, possibilities are endless. You and your parrot can enjoy going places together and even "going for a flight." However, taking the parrot outdoors is not only fun, but also a great way to socialize your parrot for improved behavior. The health and relationship benefits of going outside with a harness reward the massive effort harness training takes.

Chapter 6 Checklist:

☐ Flying is integral to parrot health both physical and mental
☐ Wing clipping causes difficult-to-solve behavioral problems
☐ Enjoy your parrot's unique ability to fly
☐ Flight safety is an important consideration for all parrots
☐ Keep windows, doors, and bathrooms closed
☐ Disable or remove ceiling fans
☐ Do not cook with parrot out
☐ Prevent interaction with other pets
☐ Do not take parrots outside without carrier or harness
☐ Do flight training by targeting between 2x training perches
☐ Replace one training perch with your hand for flight recall
☐ Teach parrot to fly back to its training perch
☐ Do daily flight training exercises to help parrot dissipate energy and improve health
☐ Have fun with flight by teaching flying tricks such as flighted fetch, fly through hoop, and boomerang
☐ Teach a parrot to wear a harness voluntarily
☐ Make sure taming prerequisites are met before introducing the harness
☐ Desensitize parrot to harness
☐ Target parrot to put on collar by itself
☐ Practice the complete harness and start going outside

Chapter 7: Trick Training & Talking

Parrot trick training is more than just a cute spectacle for your friends. Trick training is a means of achieving the best pet qualities from your parrot through learning. In the process of learning to show its wings or fetching a ball, the parrot is earning reinforcement from you as well as learning to learn. Although there is no way to convince your parrot that you are its master, you can come close to this by playing the role of teacher. The more tricks your parrot learns from you, the more eager and likely it will be to try new things. Whether it's taking medication, moving to a new home, transferring ownership, or dealing with hormones, establishing a training relationship will make these things easier to accomplish. In essence, teaching tricks is a form of enrichment and a way to maintain good training habits, while building a stronger bond.

Basics of Teaching Tricks

By now you should already know the fundamentals necessary for teaching parrot tricks. Using a clicker and a treat is the way to go. Just like target training, teaching tricks follows the same pattern of cue, behavior, clicker, and treat. Your parrot not only knows its first trick already, targeting, but also has a very basic understanding of how to earn treats from you. Teaching targeting first is not only helpful for directing the parrot where you need it for learning other tricks, but more importantly it teaches the bird how to learn from you.

Most parrot tricks come in one of four categories: target-based, captured, shaping-based, or retrieve-based. Teaching tricks across all four categories will challenge your parrot most while teaching a fun variety of behaviors. Target-based tricks are taught by using the target stick to direct the parrot to make the behavior you seek. Captured tricks are behaviors your parrot does naturally but put on cue. Shaping-based tricks involve manipulating the parrot's body to learn the behavior. Retrieve-based tricks involve the parrot picking something up and bringing it somewhere. Using these four systems, you can teach your parrot almost any trick.

Don't forget that the pace at which your parrot may learn tricks will vary. Sometimes, it may be a matter of minutes; other times, it can take weeks. The most important thing is always to make forward progress, no matter how slight. While training, try to reward the best four out of five iterations. But don't reward the worst out of five so that the parrot always strives to do better. This is a ballpark concept and shouldn't be counted out too literally. You don't want to under-reward the parrot because it may just give up. Even if the behavior isn't performed ideally, be sure to reward the best four out of five attempts. Do not click or reward failed attempts or the worst out of five. Over time the parrot will learn to do more of what earned it the treats and less of what did not. Success will be assured.

Normally, you should only teach one trick at a time. Furthermore, you should continue practicing that trick for at least a week or more before moving to the next one so that the parrot does not get confused. Previously learned tricks should continue to be practiced for life but not necessarily as vigorously as the newer ones. Do not accept a partially learned trick as completed. Keep working on it until it is done very well and then continue practicing it. This will ensure that the variant of the trick the parrot retains in its long term memory will be the proper one and not a partial variant.

Teach tricks in one or two training sessions a day when your parrot is hungriest and most motivated. Test your parrot's motivation using known tricks or targeting. If your parrot doesn't target eagerly then it is even less likely to learn anything new. Always warm up the training session with some known behavior. After warm up, go straight to teaching new tricks and save practicing old ones for the end of the session when motivation will be at less than peak levels. Also save taming exercises (such as grab training, opening wings, rolling on back, etc.) for the very end, because these require the least motivation or physical effort on the parrot's part and can still be successful with diminishing motivation. A good way to prolong peak motivation for training is to start with smaller or less desirable treats in the beginning of the training session and move toward bigger or more desirable treats as you proceed. This keeps the parrot hungry longer (small treats are less filling), but also compensates for diminishing motivation with better treats.

Training session lengths will vary depending on success. You must avoid working your parrot past its stamina for learning something new. If behavior quality is diminishing, continued training is unlikely to help. At first, a parrot unaccustomed to training may only endure a few minutes per training session. As the parrot becomes more excited about training, sessions may last as long as 30 minutes. Whatever the duration, it is the long term success of the outcome that you must always aim for. Try to end sessions on success and while some motivation is still left over, rather than fighting against poor results and diminishing responses.

If you want to teach more than one trick at a time, make sure each trick is of a different type. The two types of tricks are cued and object induced. Cued tricks are triggered by a verbal or hand cue that you make. Object induced tricks are cued by the sight of the object the parrot will be performing the trick with. Do not teach two cue tricks (like wave and turn around) at the same time or the parrot will likely get confused between the two. Instead teach tricks of differing types. Teach one that is induced by the object (such as go through tube, where the sight of the tube tells the parrot this is the trick to do) and a cued one (such as wave, in which seeing your signal tells the parrot to wave). Since the cues or objects for the tricks are entirely different, the parrot is less likely to mix up the two tricks.

Almost certainly you will hit roadblocks and plateaus in training. The first one will occur when you try to teach the second trick of the same category (particularly cue based tricks). It is a lot easier to teach a parrot that knows multiple tricks yet another trick without confusing it between the ones it already knows. However, the greatest challenge in teaching a parrot its second trick is getting it not to forget the first one. The way to ensure the smoothest possible transition through this difficulty is to make sure the prior trick(s) was fully learned and extensively practiced. Throw in a few instances of the old trick in the midst of teaching the new one to remind the parrot that these are different and both equally important. In other words, fix the damage as it happens.

If the parrot forgets the first trick or mixes up the new trick when being cued for the previous one, simply reteach the old trick using the original training techniques. This may be a bit of extra work but it's not much. Usually after a few times of relearning the prior trick, the behavior will come back much quicker than learning it originally. In this process, the parrot will learn that the new and old tricks are independent of each other and must both be learned. Going from the first to second trick will be the biggest challenge, but you may face similar trick confusion down the line. Just use the same methods for solving these issues as they happen. Things will get easier as you become more experienced at teaching and your parrot at learning.

Cues

Cues are an important element of any trick because they are the signals that tell the parrot exactly which (of many) tricks to perform. Since parrots are such avid vocalists, they tend to discern audible cues well. Make it a habit to say what you are doing whenever you are doing something with the parrot in a consistent manner. For example, when you target, say "target." When you wrap the bird in a towel, say "towel." When you take the bird out of the cage, say "want to come out?" By pairing a consistent cue with everything you do, the bird will know what is going on from the words, especially if what is being shown changes.

When teaching tricks, do the same and make a cue for all behaviors. This can be very useful when transferring a learned concept to a different object. For example, if you always say "target" when you use the target method with your parrot, you will be able to change to a different stick or your finger and say "target" to achieve the same result. Your parrot will already know what to do. This can be convenient for teaching it to touch an object you are using for a new trick by saying "target" and presenting the object.

Despite their acute awareness of audible cues, parrots are even quicker visual learners. For this reason it is best to use a visual cue as well as a verbal one. The best strategy is to begin using the verbal cue (and if possible the visual one) from the earliest stages of teaching a new trick so that the parrot has more time to get used to it. It is very helpful for the bird to learn both visual and verbal cues for all tricks to perfection because if the bird ever forgets or mixes up the cue, you can back it up with the other. Also if you ever wish to change the visual or verbal cue, you can continue presenting the known cue while also using the new one in parallel. For example, if your parrot is used to doing the wave trick when you wave your hand and say "wave", you can change it by waving and saying "hello" instead. Or you can say "wave" while holding your hand out for a handshake to make this the new cue for the trick.

Using an extensive array of cues will not only make teaching new tricks easier but also create a language of understanding between you and your parrot. Continue practicing tricks with all of the known cues. But once the trick is perfected, use only one cue at a time to keep both the visual and verbal cue practiced. If the parrot is having trouble, use both cues simultaneously. Once there is improvement, return to using one cue at a time. For tricks involving objects, it's a good idea to have a unique verbal cue for every object in case in the future you have multiple objects laid out. For example, say "go down the slide" and then "go through tube" to tell your parrot which trick to do first and then which one to follow up with. If you always say the cue when you have the bird do the trick, you'll have the best control over trick training in the future.

Target-Based Tricks

Since your parrot already knows how to target, it is very easy to teach a target-based trick first. A target-based trick is one where you have your parrot follow a target stick to learn the motion you want to teach. Some examples are: turn around, go through a tube, down a slide, or come to a certain location. You've already learned about targeting in Chapter 4, but if your parrot isn't already an expert at targeting, it is best to go back and review Chapter 4 before continuing.

The mechanism for teaching all target-based tricks is the same. You use the target stick to get the bird to come where you want and then pull the stick back at the same speed as the bird approaches to lead the motion. At the end of the motion you click and reward without letting it touch the stick. The only thing that will differ from one trick to another is the motion path or object that the trick pertains to. Eventually, just the sight of the object or a verbal/visual cue can be used to get the parrot to perform the trick without a target stick.

The turn-around trick is not only easy to teach but also fun to watch. To start the training, have your parrot stand on a training perch. Remind it of targeting by targeting it in a few directions before proceeding. Show the target stick to the parrot's side so that it would have to turn its head 90 degrees to touch it. When it does, click and reward. Next, place the stick behind but again slightly to the side of the parrot to get it to turn 180 degrees to touch the stick. After a few instances of the half turn, target the parrot 180 but then shift the stick slightly farther down the circle as the parrot is coming. If you simply place the stick at 270 degrees, the parrot will probably just be sneaky and turn 90 degrees in the opposite direction. So instead, place it at 180 and then shift it just ahead of the parrot to 270 degrees. If you are having trouble getting your parrot to turn this way, try having it turn in the opposite direction. Watch the way your parrot normally turns around on its own. They usually have a preferred direction.

This is a good time to introduce the verbal cue for the trick. Begin saying "turn around" or "spin" as you present the stick instead of saying "target" or "touch". Say the cue and start with the stick in front of the parrot (but far enough away that it cannot touch it). Keep the stick either above or below the parrot. Above is preferable but some parrots find this position frightening, in which case point the stick up from beneath the perch. Move the stick in a circular motion around the parrot keeping it just slightly out of reach so that the bird follows it. Once past the 180 degree point, the parrot's inertia will make it continue the motion to straighten out so you can remove the stick and click your clicker when the parrot completes the turn.

It won't take long before you can easily get your parrot to turn in place by following the target stick. The only remaining bit is to transfer the entire behavior to a cue in place of the stick. Hold your index finger out on the stick so it is pointing the same direction as the stick while you continue practicing. Progressively hold the target stick closer and closer to the tip until your index finger is even with the tip. After doing the turn around motion this way with the stick, try using just your finger without the stick. More than likely, out of habit, your parrot will follow your finger around the path. Keep practicing using just your finger to guide your parrot to turn around. But now, try to lure it less and less with your finger and allow it to complete the motion. Move your finger around the parrot to guide it 270 degrees, then 200, 180, 150, then 90 degrees. Eventually, just showing your finger in front of the parrot will get it started and then it will complete the turn on its own. At that point, start showing your finger higher or lower depending on which side you taught it. Make a small circular motion with your finger while saying the cue. If your parrot doesn't understand, move back a bit or revert to the target stick. But, once you are able to show the circular motion from above, start showing this ahead of the parrot instead. Do not reward the parrot if it turns around on its own without being cued, but take advantage of this by cuing it next time just before it could do it on its own so that it learns only to follow the cue. At this point you will be able to make a circular motion with your finger from wherever you stand and the parrot will turn around on its perch. Just remember to click and reward at the completion of the turn. But don't click too soon. Wait until the full 360 degrees are completed. This will be important if you later want the parrot to turn around on a flat surface so that it doesn't cheat and end the turn too soon. Keep practicing the trick until you can just say the command without having to indicate the motion with your finger.

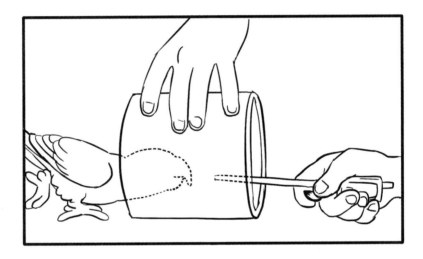

To teach your parrot to go through a tube, down a slide, or follow virtually any other course, lead it with the target stick and walk it through the motion. Progressively use the stick less and less and have a cue to get the bird started. As you phase out the target stick, the parrot will have a good idea of what to do. Avoid luring a parrot with a treat for these types of tricks because the parrot tends to learn worse when it is just going to where food is rather than following a learning procedure.

Cue-Based Tricks

There is a wide assortment of cue-based tricks that you can teach your parrot to perform on cue such as wave, shake, nod, and wings. Each trick has its own technique for teaching but then is cued with a word or gesture like any other. It is a good idea for your parrot to already be familiar with targeting and receiving treats before you teach your first cue-based trick. Since teaching parrot tricks is easier to show than to explain, I recommend referring to my DVDs (available at www.ParrotWizard.com) as well as to my free trick training guides (at www.TrainedParrot.com). But here is a very brief overview of what to expect when teaching some of these cue-based tricks.

The process of teaching a parrot to wave is basically a fake "step up" on cue. Bring your finger toward your parrot's feet as though asking it to step up. When it raises its foot to step up, you click (without allowing it the chance to actually step up) and give a treat.

To teach a parrot to shake its head, blow across the parrots ear or nose and it will reflexively shake its head. Click and reward. Show and say your shake cue as you are blowing so that it learns to demonstrate the shaking behavior when it sees the cue without even the blowing.

Essentially, any behavior can be shaped or captured and put on cue. The process for doing this is to observe the natural occurring behavior or to artificially induce it. In the beginning, you may have to show the cue, click, and reward reactively after the behavior is observed. However, with practice the bird will offer the behavior more frequently and you can try to predict it by cuing just beforehand. Since you don't reward when the behavior is offered without cue but do reward when it is cued, the parrot learns to perform it on cue only.

As for shaping behaviors, this can usually be done by targeting, luring (which is less effective than targeting), holding, pushing, touching, or otherwise manipulating your parrot's limbs or position so that the bird demonstrates the behavior you seek. Likewise, cue the behavior beforehand and click & reward once the behavior is displayed. With time, reduce the amount of shaping you have to inflict by doing it from further away, for shorter durations, with less pressure, etc. until the parrot can display the behavior entirely on its own from the cue.

Retrieve-Based Tricks

A great deal of parrot tricks are based on the retrieve, so it merits a separate explanation. Tricks such as putting rings on a peg, coins into a piggy bank, basketball, or completing a puzzle all require the parrot to pick up an object in one location and then deposit it in another. This is called the retrieve, but I prefer to just call it fetch.

To teach your parrot to fetch, you must find a suitable object that will be easy for your parrot to hold in its beak and light enough that it can carry it. For the smallest parrots such as budgies, parrotlets, and cockatiels, a mini-checkers piece is good. For small to medium parrots such as conures, Senegals, greys, and Amazons, a regular-sized checkers piece or a wiffle golf ball will do. For the larger parrots, a wiffle baseball or just about anything that the birds can hold will work.

It is easier to teach a parrot to fetch the object to a bowl prior to your hand as the bowl serves as a unique cue for where to place the object. A stainless steel food bowl from the bird's cage will often suit but sometimes a slightly bigger bowl will make it easier. The trick is best taught on a parrot training perch, so that you can hold the bowl underneath the bird to catch the object when it is dropped.

The first step in teaching your parrot to fetch is to get it to hold the object. With larger, playful parrots this is exceptionally easy. Just give the object to the parrot and it will hold and play with it. Await with the bowl below and as soon as the object falls into the bowl, click and reward. With smaller parrots that are not accustomed to holding things, this is a tricky trick to teach. They'll need to be taught to hold the object. A way to begin this is to target the bird to touch the object, then say "target" and have the bird target the object itself. Then click only for the times it touches the object for a longer time, then reward when it tugs a bit on the object to pull it out of your fingers. Eventually, this will turn into the bird flicking the object and this is progress. From there you can reward when the flick makes it into the bowl and withhold the reward when it does not. Over time, the bird will learn to flick and eventually carry the object to the bowl.

Once the parrot is holding or flicking the object, continue to teach it to put the object specifically into the bowl by click/rewarding when the object goes in and ignoring when it does not. In order to differentiate this, sometimes hold the bowl a little to the side so that if the parrot drops the object straight down, it will miss. Eventually, the bird will catch on and will hold the object until you approach with the bowl and soon after will walk over to the bowl and drop the object in.

The final step toward turning this into a trick is to teach the bird to put the object in your hand instead of in the bowl. Simply cup your hand above the bowl so that the parrot has to place it in your hand when trying to put it into the bowl. You should add a cue such as the word "fetch" when practicing, because it will be handy for teaching the parrot to fetch new objects in the future. Continue to practice until you can get your parrot to fetch things from different ends of its perch, turn to you, and even go after objects on the floor to bring to you.

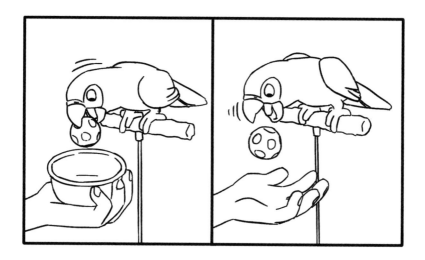

You can take fetching even further and showcase the birdness of your parrot by having it fly to you with the object from the floor. A nice trick is "whoops I dropped my keys (or change), Polly would you go fetch them for me?" Keep in mind that metallic keys or coins may be dangerous, so use plastic ones instead. If your parrot is already an ace flier, it will probably figure out what to do on its own. But in case it is not, here is the technique for teaching a parrot to fly to you with an object. Use two coffee tables or chairs set up against each other and have the parrot fetch an object from one to your hand or bowl on the other. With each successive try, spread the chairs a little further apart so that the parrot will have to walk, hop, and eventually fly across the gap. Continue increasing the gap until the parrot is making a sizable flight. Then get rid of the second chair and have the parrot fetch from the floor to the chair and eventually from the floor to your hand.

Eventually, you will be able to teach your parrot to put rings on a peg (even match them by color), play basketball (photo on page 297), put coins in a bank, or even put pieces into a puzzle using the fetch technique. Simply use the command "fetch", point to the object, cup your hand over where you want it to go and keep practicing until the parrot has it figured out. Don't forget to click and reward any attempts toward improvement.

Maintaining Tricks

The last important aspect of teaching a parrot tricks is maintaining them. Teaching a parrot a new trick only to have it forget the previous one would be counterproductive. Thus, it is important to continue practicing previously learned tricks in addition to the new ones. It is also beneficial to continue working on improving known tricks. Try to get your parrot to learn to stretch a little further, hold the pose a little longer, fetch from a little farther. The more you challenge your parrot (even when it comes to simply practicing known tricks) the better of a performer and the better of a learner it will become.

A problem you are likely to run into is confusion between tricks. Continue practicing known ones and on occasion reteach forgotten ones. Don't worry, it is easier to reteach a forgotten trick than to teach it in the first place.

As the parrot learns more tricks, you can begin chaining tricks and practicing them on variable ratio reinforcement schedules. Since the older tricks are better known and more extensively practiced, they are also effectively easier to maintain. Your parrot will offer those behaviors more readily so, over time, you can dilute the quality, quantity, and frequency of reinforcement. In other words, you can give smaller treats, less preferred treats, and not give treats every time you cue the trick for well established tricks in practice. This is a good strategy because it challenges your parrot and teaches it to perform anything you teach, including "well-behaved" behaviors, regardless of treats.

Another good reason to continue practicing known tricks regularly is that it gives your parrot an opportunity to work for food. It is believed that even for animals it is more satisfying to earn their keep than to just get it. Animals like a challenge. By continuing trick training your parrot on a daily basis, you will be giving your parrot multiple reasons to step up, flight recall, stay, come, and inadvertently perform "well-behaved" behaviors in the process. So teach lots of tricks but keep practicing them regardless of whether your parrot needs improvement or not.

Talking

Everyone enjoys seeing a talking parrot and it can be a lot of fun to show your friends. However, there are actually behavior related reasons why you should talk to your parrot and encourage it to talk. First of all, when you use words or phrases routinely, the parrot may begin to pick up on the context. Even if the bird never utters a sound, it will begin to anticipate what is to happen when you say certain things. This attention to human language is beneficial both for trick training (the parrot will be more apt at differentiating cues) and for

daily good behavior. For example walking up to the cage saying "night night" rather than "want to come out?" will signal to the bird to climb to its favorite sleeping perch rather than to come down by the door to be let out.

The more you talk to your parrot, the more likely it will learn to say those things as well. The most important reason to teach your parrot to talk (or for some species whistle) is to encourage it to make pleasant vocalizations. Otherwise, the parrot will pick up on ones you may find to be irritating. The parrot will learn to imitate some kinds of sounds no matter what, so the best defense against aggravating vocalizations is a good offense by teaching the parrot to talk.

It is important to keep in mind that some species are good talkers while others are not. Even within the same species, some parrots may learn to talk while others won't. In the scope of good behavior, the critical thing is that the parrot learns to make and get your attention with acceptable sounds. If the parrot can't talk at all but does a microwave beep and you don't mind it, give the parrot attention when it does that sound rather than when it screams. You can expect to hear plenty more where that came from and I'm not talking about the kitchen!

Encouraging Parrots to Talk

The good news is that many parrots will learn to talk entirely on their own without much effort on your part. However, it does depend on the bird hearing speech in the first place. Talking to your parrot, to other people in your household (in earshot of the parrot), and/or playing sounds from your phone or TV is a good start. Be careful though. Parrots may pick up on things you wouldn't want them to repeat so be sure to keep it PG.

Many parrots tend to pay more attention to sounds when they are in a heightened state of excitement. For those sorts of birds, it's good to play with the bird and captivate its attention while saying phrases you would like it to learn. On the other hand, some of the quieter birds pick things up in context. Saying certain things in certain situations may teach the parrot to say those things in those situations as well. For example, saying "hello" when you enter and "bye bye" when you leave may teach the parrot to greet and offer farewell to you!

Saying the same key word but in different contexts may be helpful as well. For example, if the key phrase is "pretty bird," you can say "pretty bird, who's a pretty bird? Yes, you're a pretty bird. That's a pretty bird. Pretty bird." By letting the parrot hear the phrase frequently but in exciting and differing ways can help encourage it to repeat that specific phrase.

You're not going to be able to force a parrot to say anything though. You can't use treats, training, motivation, or any of the techniques normally applied to training in order to teach the parrot to say something. These will of course later come in handy for capturing the phrases and putting them on cue. But, only the parrot can choose what specifically it will repeat. The only thing you can do is offer a variety of desirable phrases and hope that it picks up on the ones it likes.

Some parrots are very shy and only talk when they think no one is listening. Sometimes this may be going on when you're in another room or not home. It may be difficult to get this kind of parrot to talk in front of people, but you can leave the door cracked opened and try to listen. Consider running a video camera pointed at the parrot when you're gone to hear the kinds of things it is saying.

You can encourage your parrot to make more effort to talk or make pleasant noises over screaming by using positive reinforcement. If your parrot enjoys attention, you can make a greater effort to come over to the bird's cage when it is talking and not when it is screaming. You can also use food treats in a similar manner by coming over occasionally and giving treats when the parrot is chatting. This won't put the word on cue but will encourage the parrot to do more talking. When more talking is encouraged, screaming is inadvertently discouraged because the parrot can't do both at the same time.

Setting Up Phrases

When you talk to your parrot, keep in mind that anything you say may be turned back at you when the parrot starts talking. The important thing to think about when you say things to your parrot is "will it be nice if my parrot repeats it exactly this way?" For example, if the parrot's name is Frankie and you say "Frankie, what are you doing?" The parrot may learn to say exactly that phrase as "Frankie, what are you doing?" Yet, if you left out the name and just said "What are you doing?" when the parrot would say it back that way, it would sound like he's actually saying something meaningful instead of repeating straight back. Likewise, instead of saying "you're a pretty bird," say something like "hey, you're such a cutie" because if your parrot repeats that, it will sound like he's talking to a person.

In fact, you may enjoy teaching your parrot to speak so much that you'll want to teach it directed phrases. For example, you could teach it to personally greet you by saying your name.

It may be a bit unnatural at first to set the phrases by using your own name. But to make it easier, think of yourself as the parrot and what you would say then. By speaking to the parrot with phrases directed at people or phrases that are universal, you'll be able to avoid having a parrot that only speaks to itself.

Here are some good universal phrases to consider: good morning, hello, how are you, what you doing, whatsup, wanna come out, yummy, bye-bye, and night-night. If you try to say these throughout the day at every possible opportunity (but in the context of when these should be said), your parrot will be more likely to pick up on them and say them as well. If for no other reason, it's much more pleasant to come home to a parrot going "hello hello hello hello" than to a screaming parrot!

Vocalization Training Devices

There aren't many shortcuts to teaching a parrot to talk. Some pick up on talking very eagerly and others do not. However, the more talking you expose your parrot to, the better the chances that if it were to pick something up, talking would be the thing. You can purchase CDs or record yourself saying your own phrases to play to the parrot when you are not home.

Here is a neat way to expose your parrot to voices throughout the day in a less repetitive pattern. Set up 3-10 phrases from yourself or your CD on the computer. Make a blank 1 minute and a blank 10 minute recording. Put the phrases and blank recordings on an MP3 player (or simply on your computer if it is within earshot of your parrot) and play it on shuffle when you're not home. This will force breaks between words and play them at unpredictable intervals.

A simpler way to surround your parrot with voices is by leaving on the TV or Radio. However, you have no control over what your parrot may pickup then and for all you know it may be the theme song to some TV show you can't stand.

Capturing Vocalizations

Once your parrot is an unstoppable chatterbox with a wonderful collection of phrases (or for starters just a single word), you may want to be able to get the parrot to speak in public. Nearly every parrot owner has been caught with their pants down when someone begged to see the parrot talk and that is the one moment the bird acts like a mute. Wouldn't it be nice to get your parrot to say what you want when you want? This is where the process of vocalization capturing is handy.

The most basic form of capturing is simply to elicit mimicry. For a parrot that already knows a certain word or phrase, sometimes just saying it will get the parrot to say it back. Some parrots will repeat for the fun of it or to seek attention. If your parrot does not do this but you would like to encourage it, one method to try is to mimic back what the parrot says and later swap roles. When the parrot says "hello" you say "hello" back. Do this a lot and eventually say it first and see if the parrot will say it back. If the parrot does, give lots of attention. You can stop talking back and let the parrot make the responses.

A more advanced form of vocalization capturing involves taking a certain known word/phrase and getting the parrot to respond with it on cue (which can be verbal and/or visual). The process for this involves – you guessed it – clicker and treats! Your parrot should already be familiar with the clicker process from the taming and training you have done. Therefore, it should catch on pretty quickly that the click after the vocalization means a reward will be issued shortly. If your parrot is a good public speaker, this should be fairly easy. Hang onto a clicker and keep treats nearby. Whenever your parrot is around you and says the one word/phrase you are trying to capture, click and reward. If the parrot is a shy talker, you may have to stand outside the door or sit far away until it becomes talkative. When it happens to say the phrase you are looking for, click and come in to give a reward. After you do this a few times, your parrot will begin to say the phrase more frequently. Eventually, it will be saying the phrase as soon as it is done with the previous treat so that it could get another one. This is a good time to introduce the cue. Say or show the cue right after the parrot says the phrase and reward. Eventually, when you can predict that the parrot is about to say the word or phrase, make the cue first and then click/reward. This way you are tricking the parrot into having to do what it was already going to do on cue. With some further practice, you will be able to form a conversation with your parrot.

You can pretend that your parrot is a math genius by teaching it to say a single number such as "four" as the response to every question ending in "three." You can ask what is "one plus three" or "seven minus three" or "twelve divided by three." Whenever the parrot hears "three", it will know to respond "four" to get its treat. The possibilities are only limited to your imagination and your parrot's lack of lips. There are certain sounds they can't say well.

The more vocalizations you capture and put on cue, the more prone your parrot will be to learning new words and sounds down the line. By keeping your parrot talking, you are ensuring that it is less likely to scream or repeat annoying noises. Teaching your parrot to talk is another aspect of maintaining a well-rounded, fun, and well-behaved companion parrot.

Chapter 7 Checklist:

☐ Teach tricks for fun, improved learning, and better behavior
☐ Use positive reinforcement and clicker training for tricks
☐ Keep training sessions focused and quit while ahead
☐ Use verbal and visual cues for every trick
☐ Teach target-based tricks by targeting
☐ Teach cue-based tricks through shaping or capturing
☐ Teach parrot to fetch as basis for many cute tricks
☐ Practice tricks until they are saved in long-term memory
☐ Maintain known tricks with occasional practice
☐ Parrot talking is not only fun but helps drive good-behavior
☐ Use talking and vocalizations to replace screaming
☐ Expose parrot to lots of talking and sounds so it can learn
☐ You can play sounds for parrot when you are away
☐ Capture vocalizations with a clicker and put them on a cue

Chapter 8: Problem Solving

Parrots are difficult animals and no matter how correctly you handle things, you will still run into some problems. The goal is to learn about potential problems in advance and try your best to solve them preemptively. By far the easiest and most successful solution to parrot problem solving is to prevent problems in the first place.

Some of the most common problems with parrots are biting, plucking, and screaming. Solving these problems is very difficult, but there are some things owners can do to reduce these in parrots who already have them. On the other hand, preventing these problems in the first place is an inherent byproduct of following the techniques outlined in this book.

Many of the common behavioral problems found in captive parrots are the result of wing clipping. Biting, plucking, and screaming are more likely to develop in parrots that cannot fly. Flight not only offers exercise, but promotes mental stimulation, freedom, and purpose. A flighted parrot can get your attention by flying over to you, while a clipped parrot must scream. A flighted parrot can fly away from you when it is frightened but a clipped parrot resorts to biting as a last defense. A flighted parrot is preoccupied with flying around and finding things to do, while a clipped parrot ends up playing excessively with its own feathers out of boredom. I cannot stress enough how fundamental flight is to birds. When you consider all things, it becomes quite apparent that the lack of flight is a source of restlessness, neurotic behavior, aggression, and other issues. Ultimately, common behavioral problems are the direct side effects of not allowing a flighted animal to fly.

Since problems such as plucking or screaming are difficult if not impossible to reverse – while flight issues can be resolved through training – I cannot recommend any approach that does not include flight as part of the solution. For relationship and biting issues, training can solve most problems, although flight also plays a significant role as well. Thus, it is better to accept solvable problems, such as flight, over problems that may be incurable.

Biting

The most universal problem among companion parrots is biting. Nearly anyone who has ever handled a parrot has experienced a bite. While some species may be more or less prone to plucking or screaming, biting seems to happen with any and all. The good news is that most biting problems can be solved! The bad news is that there are many reasons a parrot bites and it may take some pain on your part to solve them (unless you prevent them in the first place).

Parrots bite for many different reasons. To the unaware owner, all bites seem the same and would probably be labeled aggression. In reality, parrots may bite for unexpected reasons and it may not even be because of something bad. Let's look at why parrots bite and analyze solutions for each.

The most common reason parrots naturally bite is out of fear. This can happen both intentionally as well as reflexively. The flight or fight instinct takes over in response to heightened fear and when the parrot is unable to fly away, it just bites viciously. Luckily, this is one of the easiest forms of biting to prevent and resolve. The key to preventing fear biting is to avoid eliciting severe levels of fear and to preemptively desensitize your parrot to things it may fear through socialization. With a new bird, assume that it is scared of everything and everyone. Move slowly, show things slowly, and avoid doing anything unexpected. If the bird starts to become uneasy, take things even slower. If you take things too slow, you may make less training progress. Yet, you will have prevented a biting problem from developing, which is far more valuable to the relationship.

By allowing your parrot to fly, it will more likely choose to fly away when it gets scared instead of biting. This preemptively solves many biting problems, but leaves you with some flight issues. These are more manageable and painless than biting problems and will be covered further in this chapter. By using the training methods outlined in previous chapters of this book, your parrot will learn not to fear you and in fact will look forward to your presence and thus will be less likely to bite.

If your parrot is fearful of certain objects, actions, or people, the easiest solution is to avoid exposing the parrot to them. However, the parrot may inadvertently be exposed to these which will still result in biting. So instead of sheltering your parrot from things it fears, use taming and training to slowly expose the bird to these in manageable doses. As you eliminate things from your parrot's fears, the parrot will be unlikely to take it out on you by biting.

Other times parrots bite as a way to say "no." Although the parrot is not fearful to go back into its cage, it may just not want to right now. It bites as an attempt to prevent you from making it step up or go back to the cage. In order to avoid "no" bites, instead only pose questions where the parrot can demonstrate a "yes." Teach your parrot to say yes with its actions through training. By teaching your parrot to step up by coming to your hand by itself rather than you putting your hand directly in front of the bird, the parrot can say yes by coming. The parrot does not need to bite to say "no." The lack of an affirmation by walking to your hand is a "no" by default. By respecting the parrot's "no" and finding a way to get a "yes," you will remove the parrot's use of biting to say "no."

Another type of biting is displaced aggression. Sometimes when parrots get scared of something distant, they begin biting all over and naturally hitting the closest thing to them (which most likely is you). This can occur seemingly at random. The parrot may be happily sitting on your shoulder when it spots something it is afraid of. In the state of panic, it starts biting in self-defense but this ends up hurting you. Unlike the defensive fear biting, displaced aggression is not aimed at you, yet you get accidentally caught in the midst of it. In this case, flight may help to an extent but not entirely. Certainly it helps that the parrot can fly away from your shoulder, rather than bite you when it sees a bird of prey out the window that frightens it. However, since displaced aggression may be spur of the moment, there can be times when even a flighted parrot starts lashing out rather than flying off. For this type of biting, the best solution is socialization. By exposing your parrot to as many possible people, places, objects, and situations, the likelihood of something frightening the parrot to the point of exhibiting displaced aggression is greatly reduced. Chapter 9 is entirely devoted to this process of socialization so this solution will be expanded on further.

Parrots can be naturally very possessive. Since in the wild they may have to fight with other species or members of their flock for resources, this can drive a possessive response. There are several things to do in order to diminish possessive aggression. First of all, try to avoid giving the parrot opportunities to become overly attached to objects and develop this sort of possessive attitude. For example, reaching into a parrot's cage to take out a toy may result in a bite. The parrot has become accustomed to that toy being there and your hand's intrusion is not welcome. Of course you can avoid this issue by keeping the parrot out of the cage during the toy change; however, the behavior still would go unresolved. To prevent the problem, change toys in the cage frequently. Not only does this make the parrot more accustomed to you reaching in, it also gives the bird less opportunity to become excessively attached to the toy. This example can extend to all items a parrot comes in contact with.

Flight does not help solve possessive aggression and in fact may provide the parrot greater opportunities to exhibit it. A flight capable parrot may even fly at and attack people that it deems threatening to its possessions or territory. Clipping does not solve the problem either. Eventually, someone will have to come in contact with the parrot and may still be perceived as a threat to possessions and will get bitten. For these reasons, it is imperative to deal directly with the problem.

From a training perspective, some of this possessive behavior can be mitigated by training the parrot to perform an incompatible behavior during times when it may be possessive. Back to the toy changing example; given a parrot that won't let you touch its toys, you can train the parrot to let you. Whenever you are about to change a toy, target the parrot to a certain distant perch and reward. While your parrot is busy eating, you will be able to change the toy. This will also teach the parrot to welcome toy changes, rather than get possessive, because it brings good things (such as a treat and a new toy).

Over time, you won't have to target, the parrot will simply know to step aside during the toy change and not bite.

A specific form of possessive aggression is territorial aggression. Parrots can become very defensive of not only their surrounding objects but even the very location. Territorial aggression can generally be mitigated using similar techniques as for possessive aggression. Make the parrot accustomed to you entering its vicinity and territory. Don't let it get too attached to a specific location by changing the placement of its cage periodically. Turn your (or others') entering its territory into a positive rather than undesirable event by giving treats, taking it out, and doing training. Territorial and possessive aggression share the same purpose, but by turning intrusions into opportunities, biting can be minimized.

This possessive aggression need not only apply to objects, it can apply to people as well. Some parrots may develop such a strong bond with a single person that they become possessive and attack other people that come near. For this reason it is very important not to allow a parrot to grow too attached to a single person. Socialization toward many other people is important so that the parrot knows from early on that other people exist and the bird will not always be the center of everything. For the already human possessive parrot and prior to socialization being achieved, a stationing approach similar to the one mentioned for changing toys can be used. For a parrot that flies over to bite anyone else that enters the same room as you, you can work on teaching it to station on its perch instead. For the purpose of training, have someone come into the room to the greatest extent the parrot does not react (even if it's just standing at the far end or peering through a door). At that point, target your parrot to its perch and reward. Practice this extensively so that every time someone enters the room, the parrot goes to its perch to get rewarded. Eventually, even have the stranger go over to give the reward to the parrot for being on its perch. Over time the parrot will forget about the possessiveness it used to bite for and instead will go to its perch to receive treats. Once the possessive/biting behavior is alleviated, the parrot should have learned to not attack strangers and not even require treats to continue this. Another thing a parrot can be possessive about is attention. This is where jealous aggression comes in.

A jealous parrot could end up biting the owner or other people because it is jealous of attention that is being diverted away from it to others. The parrot may start biting you out of jealousy when you engage with a friend, answer the phone, pay attention to a different pet, or get busy on your computer. Biting is the parrot's way of punishing you for diverting your attention away from it. Since parrots get bored easily, prevention is key to avoiding jealous biting. It's worth reducing situations that might cause jealousy, but the fact is that we will inevitably be too busy at times to deal with the bird. To avoid the biting resultant by jealousy, try to avoid having your parrot out when you won't be able to give it sufficient attention. Furthermore, try to ensure that the time you spend with your parrot when it is out is as fulfilling as possible. Trick training is perfect for this. Your attention needs to be on the parrot and the parrot's attention needs to be on you. When it comes to just "hanging out time" with your parrot, try to take it out at times when it is naturally more mellow such as midday, after dinner, or after training/exercise. A tired parrot is less likely to be bothered by diversion of attention than a bored, hyper one.

One type of biting that even owners with a great relationship may unexpectedly experience is biting as a result of over excitement. Things may be going great, you may be petting the parrot, and then out of nowhere you get a nasty bite. The issue is that parrots appear to experience happiness and aggression in similar ways. Basically, both of these states elicit excitement, and heightened excitement triggers biting. The body language and signs for extremely happy excitement and biting are often the same, including eyes pinning, purring, growling, and other movements. When a non-aggressive parrot becomes too excited, it simply cannot contain itself and lets out a bite. The way to avoid this type of excitement biting is to avoid over-stimulating your parrot. Instead of giving it so much petting and attention all at once, pace it out a little to avoid creating excessive excitement. Learn to read excitement body language and avoid overstepping it to the point that it results in a bite. Don't confuse this type of excitement biting with other forms. If your parrot doesn't bite except for when you make it too happy, this is the type of biting to avoid. Rough play, finger chasing, and other similar types of activity can also evoke this type of excitement biting, so it is best avoided.

Besides biting out of excitement, there is a host of nipping and playful biting that a parrot can inflict. These types of bites should not be confused with premeditated ones. Nipping is differentiated from biting in that it is less severe and usually not done with the intention of defense/attack. Sometimes the parrot thinks your skin is something interesting to chew. Nipping can range from annoying to painful. Prevent it early to avoid it from becoming rougher. For nipping, the best you can do is provide lots of toys and just wait for your parrot to grow bored of chewing you. Try to keep fingertips, ears, and other easy-to-chew bits out of reach so your parrot doesn't learn to play with them for fun. At other times, nipping indicates attention seeking and must be ignored. Most nipping can be led to extinction by ignoring it. The most important thing is not to ever reward nipping with attention and thus allow it to become learned biting (a topic which will be covered shortly). Instead of reacting to attention nipping, provide toys and activities to keep your parrot busy ahead of time before it has the chance to nip you and learn it works.

Sometimes parrots use their beak to hold on as an extra hand. In this case, try to avoid letting your parrot feel unbalanced. If the parrot is flighted, it is more likely to save itself by flying off than necessarily grabbing hard with its beak. Use a target stick to train your parrot to step up using only its feet and not lean with its beak. When a parrot leans on a person's hand with its beak to step up, this can make the person nervous. The nervous reaction may cause the person to pull the hand away and the parrot to bite out of confusion. Use the target training method outlined in Chapter 4 to teach the parrot to stretch its head upward while stepping up solely using its feet. The target stick helps direct the parrot to keep its head high while stepping up and teaches the parrot not to lean with its beak.

Hormonal aggression may occur seasonally and during adolescence. This type of aggression is normally triggered by seasonal or environmental changes that cause the parrot to enter a reproductive cycle. Most flight and training solutions are ineffective at dealing with this instinctive aggression to defend nesting sites, mates, and babies. Some people end up clipping their parrots out of frustration of not being able to deal with unpredictable aggression driven by hormones. This still isn't a solution because the parrot will eventually have to be handled and will then have the opportunity to bite. There is a solution, however. Carefully following the healthy feeding schedule (Chapter 4) reduces the state of excessive food resources for the parrot, which diminishes or prevents reproductive hormonal activity. By keeping your parrot's weight in check and its mind busy with training, your parrot will be less likely to become reproductively hormonal to the point of aggression. If it does become aggressive, try reducing calories further by diluting the diet with more vegetables, less protein, and fewer carbs.

Biting can also be reflexive. Even if your parrot never bites you, it may suddenly bite your hand if you approach unexpectedly. There are two solutions to this form of unintentional biting. First, always be careful when waking a sleeping or distracted bird. Don't just stick your hand in a cage or carrier without letting your parrot first realize that it is you. Always request a parrot to step up by showing your hand to the side rather than right in front. This gives the parrot enough time to process the request and choose to comply. If the parrot agrees to step up, it will walk over and get onto your hand by itself. If it chooses not to step up, you have been spared a bite because the parrot has been taught to say "no" by just not coming rather than biting your hand!

The other side to reducing reflexive biting is to handle your parrot as much as possible and by as many people as possible. As you go through more trick training (Chapter 7) that involves greater touching and manipulation with your hands, the parrot will become so accustomed to being held and handled that it will be less likely to get startled into a reflexive bite. These biting reflexes can be curbed, but still avoid startling your parrot unnecessarily.

This only leaves learned aggression which is arguably the most common and most threatening biting problem. Just as positive reinforcement is highly successful for teaching parrots good behavior, it is equally (if not more) successful at teaching bad behavior, such as biting. Learned biting is most preventable but very difficult to overcome once learned. Once your parrot learns that it can get what it wants by biting, it takes a very high dose of unsuccessful biting to convince it to stop trying. This is why prevention is key.

If you just acquired your parrot, whether as a baby or a rescue, you have a fundamental advantage by being able to prevent learned biting from the start. Even if you acquired a rescue parrot with a history of learned biting, it can be fairly quickly taught that biting may have controlled other people, but not you. If, unlike prior owners, you never yield to biting from the start, the parrot will realize that things are different with you.

Now is a very good time to get into what "giving in" to a bite is. Giving in or yielding to a bite occurs when the human responds to a bite in the way the parrot desires or some other way that could be desirable. Since you probably don't know what your parrot is trying to achieve by biting you, there is only one way to respond that can guarantee that the parrot is not rewarded. And that response is no response. It is essential to ignore the biting and not react or change your behavior in response to it. If you have to, you can try to free your hand or deflect the actual physical bite to save yourself. However, don't do or not do something because the parrot bit you. Don't say "no." Don't say "ouch." Don't put your parrot away. Don't spray your parrot, hit it, or walk away either. Virtually anything you do could be used against you by the parrot and could reinforce further biting. The only way to ensure that you are not doing anything to encourage future biting is to ignore it and go on as though it didn't happen. This way, over time, the parrot will learn that biting is a waste of energy because it doesn't get it what it wants anyway. Don't forget that this applies to learned or intentional biting for the purpose of manipulation. Previously described forms of biting operate differently but should still be dealt with in a similar "ignore" manner to avoid reinforcing them further. For example, leaving your fearful parrot alone when it starts biting, not only reinforces biting but also encourages it to be more fearful around you in the future. Saying "no," making any other sound, or even performing any action can teach your parrot to bite you on purpose just for laughs. It's like pulling a string on a doll to make it talk, the parrot learns that it can get cheap laughs by biting you and watching you complain.

A great example of the duality of learned biting and why it must be ignored is about going back to the cage. A parrot could bite you when you try to put it away into the cage to avoid going back. But even that same parrot can learn to bite you when it wants to go back. For example, if you try to "punish" your parrot by putting it away in the cage whenever it bites, the parrot can learn to bite you whenever it actually wants to go back to the cage. On the flip side, if you yield to a parrot that bites to avoid being put away, it will learn to always bite you when you try to put it away so it could stay out longer. Even if you don't change your actions in response to these bites but say "no" or "don't bite," the parrot may learn to bite just to make you talk. Sometimes parrots bite to be left alone while other times they do it for attention. Bites, therefore, can serve different purposes and any response could potentially encourage more biting. For all of these reasons, avoid making any response and ignore biting by going on doing what you were going to do. However, if your parrot bit you right before you were going to give it a treat, don't give the treat or it will appear to be a response to the bite.

Far more important than ignoring the bite when it happens is preventing bites from happening in the first place. In fact, any stimulus associated with a bite could potentially encourage the parrot to bite more frequently, even if it's just for the thrill of pinching skin. If bites are extensively avoided in the first place, then the parrot has no way of learning that bites can be effective. Ways to prevent biting are described all throughout this book without explicitly stating so. By target training your parrot, diverting its attention with treats, teaching tricks, setting up food schedules, etc., you are already teaching your parrot things to do other than bite and means of getting treats/attention from you without ever laying beak to skin. The well-behaved parrot strategy already encompasses a system for preventing biting in the first place. It teaches the parrot how to get what it wants in ways that do not cause the bird to revert to biting.

Screaming

Screaming is about as natural to parrots as biting is. As with biting, parrots scream for many different reasons. They can scream for attention, in defense, to communicate, out of boredom, from excitement, or even from excessive energy.

Also, as with biting, the methods recommended throughout this book are aimed at preventing screaming in the first place. Allowing parrots to fly in your home discourages screaming because they can simply fly over to you instead. Healthy feeding prevents excessive energy that gets let off through screaming. Training and flight provide exercise that tire a parrot and reduce screaming. Performing tricks or talking gives the parrot a means of soliciting attention in an acceptable manner instead of screaming.

The first step to resolving screaming is to realize that a certain level of screaming is completely natural in a parrot and can probably never be eliminated. This will vary from species to species with some typically being quiet while others being extremely noisy. Realize what the natural level of noise-making for your parrot is and set *that* as your target, not absolute silence. The goal is to avoid and reduce learned screaming. Natural screaming is unlikely to go away.

One of the biggest reasons parrots learn to scream or make a lot of noise is to seek attention. Since they are locked away in cages or unable to fly, they rely on humans, both for support and entertainment. By minimizing this dependence and giving the parrot more freedom, screaming can be reduced. Providing toys, foraging opportunities, and other things to keep the parrot occupied can help as well. These will be discussed in Chapter 10. Ultimately these can become boring as well. The remaining solution is to provide ample out of cage time, flight, and training. These activities keep the parrot busy and stimulated and thus reduce screaming.

The best strategy to reduce screaming during times when you are busy is to keep the parrot caged in a separate room or area. Ideally, this area should be both visually and audibly isolated from where you are located. If the parrot cannot hear or see you, it will eventually realize that screaming is futile and will give up. However, if you keep the parrot closer to you, the screaming will become unbearable and you may eventually give in and give the parrot the attention it craves. Even if you don't give in to screaming, the parrot may be more tempted to continue trying if it senses your presence nearby. For these reasons, when you are unable to devote attention to your parrot, cage it in a solitary location with lots of toys to keep it occupied.

To prevent a parrot from learning to scream for attention, it is very important to ignore screaming and never do anything in response to it. While biting can often be prevented, parrots will scream naturally from time to time. The main way to keep that from becoming more frequent is to avoid responding to it. A shout of "be quiet," a slam of the door, or a squirt of a bottle may encourage the parrot to scream even more. Any attention is better than nothing for a bored animal. Alleviating boredom and ensuring that screaming is not rewarded is the most effective method for keeping learned screaming to a minimum.

Another strategy for preventing or reducing attention-seeking screaming is to respond only to vocalizations. If your parrot says something in its cage or makes a noise that is less unpleasant, you should go up to the cage and give attention or take the parrot out. By giving the parrot a sound that earns it attention, you will give the parrot a less aggravating way of calling for you. This also encourages your parrot to do more talking.

If your parrot is a particularly adept talker, you can teach it to say "let me out" or something like that. Whenever you naturally go to let your parrot out, say the phrase "let me out." Over time your parrot may start to say it on its own as a vocalization. But to teach the context, whenever the parrot says it, go and let it out for a little bit. Over time, the bird will be able to ask to come out. From thenceforth you don't have to always respond to the vocalization by letting it out. Simply take it into consideration and occasionally make the effort to let it out when it asks. Since your parrot will inevitably make it known when it wants to come out, it is best to encourage the parrot to do this with a noise you find less annoying.

    The last way to quiet an extremely noisy parrot is through training. If you have a parrot that has learned to be excessively noisy, here is a way to reduce this. Instead of feeding meals at mealtimes, you will need to feed when the parrot is quiet. For maximum effectiveness, feed a single or a few pellets out of your bird's daily portion at a time. Do not give anything when the parrot is noisy. When the parrot is silent for a sustained length of time (at first this may be a short span of time but as things improve, wait longer and longer), walk in and drop the pellet(s) in its food bowl. If the parrot starts screaming as you approach, turn around and walk away. Since the parrot will only receive food when it is silent or at least makes a pleasant vocalization, it will eventually have to learn to make less noise. Since the pellets will be drawn out a little at a time throughout the day, the parrot has to learn to spend more time being quiet. As long as the parrot is on a suitable healthy feeding regime, it will always want some more food so the strategy should remain effective throughout the day.

    By implementing these strategies as well as the system presented throughout this book, you will be able to keep your parrot's screaming to a tolerable minimum. There is no guarantee that you will eliminate all screaming/vocalization, but at the very least you can keep it from getting out of control. By teaching your parrot to talk for attention instead of screaming, the problem will be reduced.

Plucking

Feather plucking is one of the least understood problems in captive parrots. Plucking is a form of self-mutilation behavior that refers to a parrot damaging its own feathers. It can range from over-preening their feathers to entirely ripping them out. What could possibly lead such gorgeous creatures to mutilate themselves in such a horrid way? The answer appears to lie partly in genetics, partly in health condition, and mainly in behavior. Curing feather plucking can be anywhere from difficult to impossible, so it is very important to prevent it in parrots that don't already do this. By allowing a parrot flight, training it tricks, giving it attention in a predictably responsive way, enriching the environment, and giving the parrot meaning in its life, plucking should be unlikely to occur. Following the tips throughout this book should help give a parrot that meaning that will prevent it from turning to plucking. However, here are some more tips for plucking prevention.

The health status of your parrot may play a role in feather plucking, so ensuring top health is important. Health starts with your parrot's diet. Ensure that your parrot is fed a quality pellet diet in the proper quantity. Seek avian veterinarian health inspections of your parrot periodically. If there is any deficiency or health issue, it is best to catch it before it could lead to something like plucking. Allow your parrot flight and ample exercise so it remains in top shape. Flighted parrots are far less likely to develop feather plucking issues than clipped or flightless ones.

Attention and the way you give it can also play a role in causing or preventing feather plucking. Some parrots have been known to take on feather plucking after being rehomed, losing a mate, when owners leave on vacation, or some other change in attention levels. One common piece of advice is to avoid giving your parrot excessive attention early on if you cannot maintain that same level for life. This certainly holds true and you should not give more attention than you can reasonably continue to provide. However, since human schedules will inevitably change at some point and parrots live for so long, it is important to prepare them for these kinds of changes. Some day you may be more busy or need to leave on business and the parrot will have to be able to cope with attention deprivation in a reasonable manner and not resort to plucking.

To prepare your parrot to be able to handle changes in attention levels, it is important to expose it to these types of changes in a controlled manner in advance. While it is generally good to maintain a predictable schedule with your parrot, it is also good practice to occasionally break away from routine. One day, don't come home at your regular time to play with your parrot but enjoy going out instead. Some Saturday or Sunday, take the day off instead of spending it at home with your parrot. On yet another day, take your parrot out with you. By exposing your parrot to these kinds of changes in moderation from the start, the parrot is far less likely to develop abandonment issues when you are gone on vacation or if the parrot may require a new home. Don't wait until the day before you are ready to leave on vacation to discover that the parrot can't cope with your absence. Prepare the parrot by leaving it alone for progressively longer periods.

There are a few handy ways to practice this type of solitude starting with simply not taking your parrot out of its cage on some days. I am not discouraging you from taking your parrot out as much as possible; however, if you are very regular about taking your parrot out, then intentionally don't on occasion. Even if you have no need to go out, on one or two days a month, just don't let the bird out at all. This is not only preparation for when you are away but is also an experiment to see whether your parrot starts plucking if it is locked away for a little longer than usual. If you spend all day with your parrot or take it with you everywhere, you must occasionally leave the parrot home so that it does not become so attached that it cannot cope without you. This is imperative for maintaining a well-behaved parrot and ensuring that the parrot will be able to handle stress in a reasonable manner without plucking.

Before you decide to leave on a two week vacation, make sure you have been able to leave your parrot a night, day, and a long weekend before going all the way. Leave ample toys and good care and rest assured that with this adequate preparation your parrot's plumage will still be intact when you return.

Now when it comes to dealing with a parrot that is already a plucker or developing a plucking habit, there are a few tricks you can use to try to reduce it. But first it is very important to consult an avian veterinarian to ensure that this behavior isn't the result of a treatable disease, infection, or environmental problem in your home. Once you are certain that the problem is behavioral and not physiological, you can proceed to use training to try to reduce it. By far the most important thing is not to react to feather plucking! Any attention or response you make to plucking (even if it makes the parrot stop right that moment) will only encourage more of it in the future. As painful as it may be to sit and watch a parrot pluck, you must be strong about not reacting. Instead, create other means by which the parrot can seek your attention. Respond to vocalizations and give your parrot opportunities to practice tricks. Ensure that you provide ample daily attention and interaction, but not so much that your parrot is entirely dependent on you. Although I generally prefer to recommend trick training over foraging (because trick training improves the human-parrot relationship, while foraging does not), in the case of a plucking parrot, foraging is a good option to consider. The busier you can keep a plucking-prone parrot, the less opportunities it has to turn to itself and destroy feathers.

With some of the worst cases of long term pluckers, there may simply be nothing you can do to make them stop. If you have tried all medical, dietary, and training options (as well as a lot of patience, because feathers don't grow back over night), you may have to just accept that your parrot will always remain plucked. All you can do is take good care and ensure that your parrot receives a loving and fulfilling life despite its feather condition. If you continue treating it with dignity and the care that a non-plucking parrot should get, you will already make a colossal impact on its life.

Since plucking is so difficult to resolve, it is especially important to preemptively train and handle your parrot in ways to prevent plucking from developing. By providing flight, training, good diet, suitable lifestyle, avian veterinary care, ample attention, schedule variations, and meaning to its life you should have a high likelihood of preventing plucking from occurring in the first place.

Hormonal Problems

The onset of hormones can turn even the sweetest parrot into a mean green attacking machine. Most hormonal activity in parrots is seasonal and related to reproductive activity. The exact cuing of these hormones may depend on seasonal or environmental changes. Regardless of the cause, it will be necessary to be able to deal with these unpredictable urges and work through them.

Dealing with hormonal activity is an important part of maintaining a well-behaved parrot. Avoiding encouragement of hormonal behavior, controlling environment to limit hormonal triggers, and working through the behavioral issues as they come – are all part of getting through these issues. Baby parrots are not likely to exhibit any of these problems, however, as the parrot goes through adolescence they will appear. Luckily, as the parrot enters adulthood, hormonal issues will be seasonal and not all the time.

There are many ways in which hormonal behavior may be exhibited and will also vary by species. Some common displays include regurgitation, mating dances, head bobbing, excessive excitement, nest searching, nest making, and rubbing on objects or people. In female parrots, excessive hormonal activity can lead to infertile egg laying. In some cases, this can lead to egg binding and cause injury or death to the parrot. For health and behavior reasons, hormonal activity must not be encouraged and should be dealt with as much as possible.

Hormonal activity can also lead to major aggression. As a parrot develops a nesting site (possibly its own cage), it will viciously defend its territory. Furthermore, the hormonal parrot becomes extremely defensive of its mate (which may or may not be the owner) which can cause aggression toward other people. By reducing triggers for hormones, you can thus avoid a lot of the nasty behavior that comes along with it. It will also reduce the frustration your parrot feels in its lack of success mating and raising offspring.

Daylight duration, temperature, humidity, and food availability play a large role in triggering seasonal hormonal activity. The more of these variables you can consistently keep constant year round, the more control you will have over preventing the onset of hormones. Daylight duration can easily be controlled by using light bulbs to supplement darkness and covering the cage at night. By giving a parrot 12 hours of sleep every single night, you will avoid the span of daytime trigger. By using heating and air conditioning to keep the same temperature year round you will remove the temperature triggers. By using air conditioning and a humidifier (during excessive dryness), you can keep humidity in check as well. By keeping these factors fairly constant throughout the year, you are less likely to cause multiple or continuous cases of hormonal activity.

Perhaps the most significant factor for reproductive hormonal activity is excess food availability. Without excess food, a parrot cannot lay eggs and raise chicks. In the wild, during years of poor food availability, birds will skip laying eggs. Likewise, by limiting your parrot's food intake just to the amount sufficient to sustain itself, you will be able to reduce the triggering of hormones. Freefeed or an increase of caloric/nutritional value can be a hormonal trigger. For these hormonal reasons, food management becomes an equally valuable strategy for preventing the onset of hormonal behavior as for maintaining motivation for training.

When a parrot does exhibit forms of mating behavior such as regurgitating or a mating dance, it is very important not to encourage this. Some people think its cute or that their parrot is showing them affection. However, encouraging this is a problem because the parrot will never get what it seeks which will lead to frustration and aggression. If certain kinds of petting or touching lead a parrot toward reproductive behavior, it is very important to stop and not do more of this. If a parrot starts offering reproductive behavior on its own, it is important to ignore it or walk away. If a parrot's advances never succeed, it will eventually make less of them. On the other hand, if they are supported, then the parrot may start laying eggs or become more aggressive as part of the hormonal process.

Avoid stimulating reproductive hormonal behavior, and the territorial aggression that can come with it, by eliminating potential nest or nest-like sites. Keep in mind that most parrot species are cavity dwellers. Tight dark wooden holes resemble nests to them. Do not let the parrot play in drawers, baskets, or boxes. Some people think it is cute to allow their parrot to shred up a box to build a nest inside, but this will only lead to frustration or aggression when the parrot cannot succeed in mating and reproducing. Bird tents for the cage should also be avoided for the same reasons. The availability of potential nest sites is often a trigger for hormonal behavior.

Parrots tend to get mean and grouchy when they are going through their hormonal period. The best strategy for dealing with this is training. Practicing already known behaviors is a good way to get your parrot to snap out of the hormonal mood and return to good behavior that it already knows. Practice targeting, step up, and recall before your parrot has a chance to get hormonal. Then when it does become hormonal and aggressive, you can return to methods it already knows and use food as motivation to stick to good behavior rather than reproductive behavior.

Sometimes, parrots will appear to lose their tameness during adolescence or relapses of hormonal behavior. Suddenly the sweet parrot will bite rather than step up and be impossible to handle. By preemptively using the training and taming techniques outlined in this book, you will be able to quickly retrain the bird using the same methods to remind your parrot of the benefits of cooperation. Since the parrot knows these things from before, learning them again will be easy. On the flip side, trying to teach a parrot to step up for the first time while it is undergoing hormonal changes is a really bad time. So even if you have the sweetest baby that will step up without a target stick, go through the process of the training regardless so that if/when the bird is hormonal, you have a familiar process to return to. Help your parrot prioritize training over reproduction by continuing the healthy feeding routine (Chapter 4).

Since hormonal behavior cannot be controlled directly, it is important to indirectly prevent it through keeping a stable environment year round and managing food resources. By ensuring that the parrot stays busy focusing on its own survival (training and managed feeding), you can end up discouraging the hormones that drive reproductive behavior and the problems associated with it. Avoid encouraging hormonal behavior as it happens and return to training basics to get your parrot back to being as well-behaved as before.

Adolescence

The toughest part of parrot ownership in many cases is when the parrot is going through adolescence. It can also be called "terrible twos," although it does not necessarily happen at two years old in all species.

Generally speaking, smaller species will go through adolescence from 1-2 years old. Medium parrots around 2-4. And large parrots can have it go on for years ranging from 2-6 years old.

Adolescent behavioral troubles often strike suddenly but sometimes can develop gradually. Oftentimes, owners will recall the sudden turning point in their relationship with their once friendly baby. It could be a mistake the owner made such as accidentally stepping on the bird's tail, pinching it with the cage door, or being forceful with the bird. Other times, it could be more indirect such as dropping the food bowl and making a loud noise. Seemingly minor disturbances can trigger major relationship changes at this delicate age. Oftentimes, these situations are the catalyst and not the cause of the relationship changes that follow.

More often than not, adolescent parrot behavioral problems are diagnosed by the owner's anecdotal story that starts with "I had my parrot since he was a baby but ever since _____ happened, he stopped stepping up for me" or "he started biting me" or even "he stopped coming out of the cage." By the time I hear this, I already suspect the bird's age but ask just in case. When the bird's age falls into that adolescent range relative to the size, it all comes together. Situations that most adult parrots or baby parrots would overcome, end up being the catalyst for pivotal relationship changes in adolescent parrots.

No matter how hard you try, no matter how much your baby parrot likes you, no matter how much training you do, it may still not be enough to prevent these behavioral changes during adolescence. The changes can include refusing to step up, refusing to come out of the cage, switching preference for a different family member, developing biting, losing interest in training, and just all around turning wild. Unexpected and pretty random changes in personality from day to day are another symptom of adolescence. One day your parrot is good, the next it is biting, the next it seems good again, and on and on. The first step in dealing with adolescent parrot behavioral trouble is to become aware of it.

While in most stable adult parrots, the parrot's behavior is a pretty direct reflection on your interactions and training, adolescent behavior has no rhyme or reason. During this age, the parrot is very conflicted between being a helpless/cooperative baby and being an independent adult. Like teenagers, adolescent parrots can have mood swings, personality changes, and become rebellious against parents/authority. Oftentimes, the parrot may rebel against the person who took care of it as a baby and start showing preference for a different family member. All of these symptoms of parrot adolescence can be quite upsetting for the person whose pet the bird is. Especially after a period of good relations and even successful training, it can be quite hurtful when the parrot wants nothing to do with you.

Awareness of these adolescent problems is the most important part of dealing with them. When you are aware that the reason the parrot (that was once good with you) is now suddenly the opposite is because of the age and not because of something you did, it is much easier to work through it. When you take it less personally, you can behave more rationally.

The most important thing to avoid doing during these "troubled teen" times for the bird is being pushy. It can be all too tempting to demand the uncooperative bird to step up, try to punish the bird for biting, or force the parrot to spend time out of the cage when it does not want to. However, when the bird already has internal age changing hormones that turn it against you, reaffirming to the bird that you are "bad" is the worst thing to do. It becomes a self-fulfilling prophecy where the bird is already hung up on the catalyst and expects bad things from you and you reaffirm that to the bird by being pushy.

Take it easy. Don't be pushy, especially when the parrot is feeling conflicted during this troubled age. Be more mindful of the parrot's choices. If the parrot is normally good about coming out of the cage but on certain days during adolescence does not want to, leave it be. If the parrot does not want to step onto your hand, instead of nudging the bird onto your hand, find a better treat to entice it to step up.

Continue to follow the entire approach outlined in this book. Unfortunately, during a bad case of adolescence, doing everything right will barely work! It is very disappointing when so much effort brings so little results. However, it is important to be the adult and continue doing the right things even when the parrot is giving little cooperation back. Your perseverance during this time will pay off greatly when the parrot exits adolescence and matures into a well-rounded adult parrot. Those lessons that seemingly did not sink in during adolescence will surface when the bird matures.

The only true antidote to adolescent misbehavior is time. Training progress during this age will be slow. It is likely that the adolescence will end quicker than the training delivers results. And, as the bird reaches maturity, training will again become effective as with any adult parrot. Work through adolescence patiently and don't give up. Behavior will be more straightforward once the parrot matures.

You will best realize what adolescent behavior was, when the bird matures and it ends. Once conventional behavior improvement starts to clearly work again, you will look back and realize the period your bird was going through was adolescence. Hard work and patience during this period will pay off because when the parrot matures, good-behavior will stick for the long run. You can bypass the difficulty and frustration of dealing with adolescence by adopting an already matured parrot. If you get a baby parrot, be prepared to work through adolescence.

Parrot Bonds to Other Person

It is not uncommon for one member of the family to get a parrot and then be disappointed when the bird bonds to someone else. For example, wife gets an African grey as a baby, prepares delicious food, cleans the cage, and nurtures the bird, but the parrot bonds with the husband who doesn't care instead. Who a parrot will bond with is not always predictable. You may be able to have some influence over it, but it is not something you can control.

One thing that can discourage your parrot from bonding with you is being pushy or being the "naysayer." This can be tough because usually the primary caretaker is the one that wants to bond with the parrot, but being the caretaker also involves responsibility. The primary caretaker has to take the parrot out, put the parrot away, stop the parrot from doing something dangerous, etc. This creates more opportunities for the primary caretaker to be seen as pushy and drive the parrot to bond with another member of the household that doesn't seem to care.

To prevent this problem, it is very important to make sure that you only hold positive interactions with your parrot and request rather than demand behavior. Request the parrot to step up and allow the parrot to choose to step up or not to. Use rewards and incentives for the parrot to comply rather than force if it does not. Rather than snatching things away from the parrot that it shouldn't chew on and being a party pooper, hide those things in advance to prevent this situation. Offer good things to your parrot through positive reinforcement training.

Ultimately, the bird may develop a natural bond with who it chooses. You may be able to encourage it to go a certain way, but you cannot force it. If the bird bonds with a different person, all is not lost. You, as well as every other member of the household, can still develop a friendly relationship with the parrot by using positive reinforcement training and following the complete methodology outlined in this book.

Prevention

Prevention of bad behavior is the name of the game. Bad behavior can be prevented in two ways. First, you can prevent bad behavior from being learned by not giving it the chance to happen in the first place. Secondly, you can reduce bad behavior by encouraging good behavior. The more time you spend working on good behavior (including trick training, taming, playing with toys, and the other processes mentioned throughout), the less chance there is for bad behavior to pop up in that time. Basically good behavior can cancel out bad behavior and bad behavior can be reduced by not giving it the chance to happen in the first place.

When it comes to biting, if you handle your body and parrot in ways that don't give the bird an opportunity to bite you, there is no chance that you will be teaching the parrot to bite. The more time you spend around your parrot during which it does not bite you, the less inclination the parrot will have to bite you. If bites are prevented from happening in the first place, the parrot can't learn your weak spots and how to manipulate them. By using hands-off target training and progressive taming, you give your parrot time to learn what to do and prevent opportunities for biting to occur. As the parrot becomes accustomed to doing the right things, biting may not even cross its mind.

Since a parrot can often find inherent reinforcement in bad behavior, the only way to keep that behavior from self-reinforcing is to prevent it in the first place. Parrots may learn to enjoy the texture of chewing your skin but if you avoid it from happening in the first place, the habit won't have the chance to develop. Parrots become accustomed to routines and places, so if you prevent your parrot from going outside these limits long enough, it is likely to not even want to. For example, I have boxes full of bird toys open and stacked near my parrot's cages and yet my parrots never fly over to pillage them. Why not? Because the parrots are used to seeing them but never had the chance to get into them for years. Now I can keep the boxes open and they don't bother doing anything to them. The birds are so used to those boxes being something to see but not something to do. If I had placed them on that box just once or they found their own way into them, they may always want to do that. But when certain behaviors are prevented long enough, they become habit. Getting your parrot into the habit of not biting, not screaming, and not plucking is an excellent preventative measure. The way to enact this prevention is to train behavior that is incompatible.

One common preventable problem parrot owners experience is parrots being unstoppable from climbing onto shoulders. The parrot will run up a person's arm onto their shoulder and then refuse to come off. This becomes a difficult issue to solve once a parrot has become accustomed to being able to do this itself. Likewise, it is very difficult to teach a parrot to stop chewing on your ear when it is on your shoulder. Yet the most effective solution to solving these shoulder problems is to prevent your parrot from going on your shoulder in the first place. Once your parrot loses the habit of being on your shoulder, you can teach it how to be on your shoulder properly. You can place your parrot on your shoulder briefly (possibly as a reward for good behavior) and then have it step off to perform a trick and earn a treat. By allowing the parrot to spend progressively more time on your shoulder but always removing it before it gets nippy, the parrot learns the way to be on your shoulder that does not involve nipping your ear. Since the parrot is accustomed to ending up on your shoulder only by you putting it there, it doesn't try to go up there on its own. Likewise, if your parrot is only accustomed to being let out of the cage for talking, accustomed to getting treats only for doing tricks, accustomed to spending time only on parrot stands (including cages and trees), and accustomed to only chewing on parrot toys, then it will continue doing these things out of habit and be much less likely to engage in undesirable behavior.

Flighted Problems

Although there can be problems associated with keeping flighted parrots, they are actually more manageable and less severe than the side effects of clipping. The side effects of clipping such as biting, plucking, and screaming are often difficult to impossible to solve post-factum. Yet most issues related to flight can be solved environmentally or through training. Basically, you as an owner have much greater possibility to be able to control flight than something like plucking.

Possibly the greatest fear of every parrot owner when it comes to flight is that their parrot will use flight to flee rather than approach its owner. Parrot owners are wary of allowing flight because they fear that if given the choice, the parrot will prefer not to be with them and be hard to handle. When an already clipped parrot is near impossible to handle, bites, and is problematic it is not surprising that the owner would think that given flight, this parrot would stay as far away from them as possible. However, with the methods encouraged throughout this book your parrot should learn to want to be around you regardless of whether it can fly or not. By providing the proper encouragement, you will be able to develop such a good relationship that given the chance to fly, your parrot will likely use flight to come to you instead of flying away.

Flight ends up providing better and more painless feedback to the owner compared to biting. At that point all that is left is some training and the flight issue as well as fear can be solved. Also there is less chance of the owner pushing a flighted parrot beyond its fear threshold as it will fly before that threshold is reached. This reduces the likelihood of developing psychological problems.

When it comes to parrots crashing into things or being able to land in places you don't want, refer to Chapter 6 on how to safely bird proof your home. By configuring the household environment as safe for flight, those issues are directly prevented. The more you encourage and reward your parrot for spending time on bird approved locations (cage, tree, stand, etc), the more it will prefer to go to those places rather than landing on places you don't want it to go. Don't forget the concept of prevention when it comes to places you don't want your parrot to go. If you never put your parrot on your couch, it is less likely to develop a desire to go on it.

Other flighted problems are behavioral and may include flying away from the owner, not wanting to go back into the cage, being impossible to get a hold of, landing on inappropriate places, flying to attack people or pets, searching for nest sites, landing on places to destroy, and other issues specific to the parrot having the freedom to fly. Most of these issues are preemptively solvable by using the approaches outlined throughout this book. If you follow the healthy feeding plan, it will ensure that the parrot is always happy to take a treat when it is out and will be willing to cooperate. If you let a very full or freefed parrot out to freefly at home, there is obviously no reason for it to allow you to put it away. However, if the parrot is ready for a scheduled meal, it will accept being put away for food. Healthy feeding schedule, recall training practice, and well-formed habits provide a good safety mechanism in case a flighted parrot were to accidentally get outside. When the bird is hungry enough to desire to eat, you have a better chance of getting it to fly back down to you from a tree. The flight recalls you had practiced in training will be familiar and in times of hunger, the bird will remember to respond in a similar manner. If a very full bird slipped out, it may take hours or days until it is hungry enough to cooperate for food.

To reduce your parrot landing on furniture and other undesirable places, it is important not to leave anything out that the parrot can enjoy playing with. If the parrot lands on your desk and finds a goldmine of pens, papers, and other exciting things to chew, it will only want to keep coming back. Since parrots often like to imitate their human owners and play with the same things, it is important for you to show interest in parrot toys rather than human toys when the bird is out. A very common complaint from parrot owners is that all their parrot wants to do is chew up their phone or keyboard. Well, it is obvious that if the person is constantly sitting at the computer when the parrot is out, the parrot just wants to join in, because that's the thing to do! If instead of taking your parrot out when you are busy, you take your parrot out when you can devote one-on-one time, you will be far less likely to encourage undesirable behavior.

Sometimes a parrot lands on top of book cases, curtains, or other undesirable places because it doesn't have a better place to go. Place parrot trees, stands, or perches in different areas of your home so that your parrot has an approved place to land rather than on furniture. You can't expect your parrot to spend all of its time on just a single cage or tree. People have different chairs, couches, and places to go, and if you want to keep the parrot off of them, give the parrot its own bird furniture (Chapter 10). The reasons for keeping parrots off of people's furniture are not only to maintain order but also to prevent them from pooping on and chewing it up. Just remember to avoid making a big deal and giving attention if a parrot does land in an inappropriate place or the parrot will keep doing this for attention. It is all too common that a person gets busy at their TV or computer and the parrot is bored. The parrot tries to get your attention but is unsuccessful. So instead it gives you a bite or flies over to some place you don't want it to go. Suddenly, this pries you away from what you are doing even if for a little bit. This sure beats having you go on doing your own thing and giving no attention. For this reason, it is important to prevent a parrot from having a chance to misbehave in the first place. By providing many perches and parrot toys ahead of time, you have a better chance of keeping the parrot in the right places. Furthermore, get the parrot very accustomed to being in those places through training and spending a lot of time with the parrot in those areas and then it will voluntarily go there.

Chapter 8 Checklist:

- Parrots can be difficult and have problems even when you are doing a great job so don't be discouraged
- Wing clipping causes more problems than it solves
- Biting can happen for many reasons
- Avoid causing fear biting by preventing fear
- Do not cause parrot to bite to say "no"
- Prevent biting by giving parrot a way to say "yes"
- Socialize your parrot to reduce displaced biting
- Teach alternative behavior to avoid possessive biting
- Do not over-excite your parrot to avoid excitement biting
- Prevent nipping by giving alternative things to play with
- Prevent hormonal aggression by reducing hormonal triggers
- Keep sleep schedule, healthy feeding schedule, and environment consistent to mitigate hormonal triggers
- Avoid causing a parrot to bite reflexively
- Don't accidentally teach learned biting; teach alternative ways for parrot to get what it wants
- Accept that screaming is natural to parrots
- Reduce excessive screaming by managing energy levels, sleep, healthy feeding, exercise, and training
- Teach a parrot to talk or vocalize to get your attention
- Most effective solution to plucking is preventing it
- Try to use toys, foraging, training, and alternative ways to get your attention to resolve existing plucking
- Avoid providing nests or nest-like areas
- Patiently work through parrot adolescence
- Parrot may bond with other people; use training to be friends
- Prevent rather than punish unwanted behavior
- Solve flight problems with healthy feeding, training, lifestyle

Chapter 9: Socialization

Socialization is a very broad term for all of the objects, people, places, and situations that a parrot can be exposed to in order to develop a good attitude toward them. Socialization is the epitome of the well-behaved parrot approach and is the ultimate goal. Healthy feeding, flight, training, and other elements are necessary to properly execute socialization. Socialization ultimately turns a feathered wild beast into an outstanding pet that you and others can enjoy. It is a lifelong process and must be maintained. By continuously exposing a parrot to things, people, places, and situations, you are preparing the parrot for all unforeseen future experiences. The more socialized a parrot becomes, the less fearful it will be. When you eliminate fear, you also eliminate fear biting.

A parrot that has become too accustomed to monotony will have a lot of difficulty coping with changes. A parrot that has only been eating a certain food all its life will be extremely difficult to persuade to try a new food. At some point, you may wish to introduce healthier foods or change the diet when a manufacturer goes out of business. If a parrot has become too attached to its specific cage, replacing the cage can cause excessive stress to the bird. A parrot that has never been to any home but yours can develop major problems when many years later you need to move to a new home. Most parrots are never taken outside so the entire world they know is their cage and room. The rest of the world is entirely beyond them. Just imagine how terrifying it would be for a child to end up outside after spending ten years without leaving the home.

Like with food, objects and places, a parrot can become too accustomed to the people around it and be unable to cope with being around other people. The parrot may get terribly scared or aggressive around other people. Either way, this is a major problem. Even if you don't ever plan to rehome your parrot, there may come situations in life where the bird has to be around other people.

The parrot's owner could end up becoming ill or injured, have to take care of someone, travel on business, board the bird during vacation, or even just have guests over. It is inevitable that the parrot will have to be around other people at some point in its life. The owner may get married, have children, add roommates, or have some household change that brings unexpected people into the parrot's life. Instead of teaching a parrot to accept a certain specific person, the best strategy is to socialize the parrot to like people in general. This ensures that the parrot will accept any person at any time when needed.

There will be a plethora of unexpected situations that your parrot will have to encounter in its life. Whether it's going to the vet, moving to a new home, having a power blackout, or being rehomed, the parrot is best prepared for unforeseen situations by being exposed to as many possible different situations in its life in advance. A parrot that is used to dealing with unpredictable events will be much more prepared to take life's changes as they come. This chapter will cover socialization methods that are not only the road to a well-behaved parrot but also fun to do in the process.

Introducing Objects

Parrots are known to get phobic around new things. Be it new foods, toys, furniture, hairdos, or new parrot supplies, parrots will often be very cautious and possibly even petrified.

Many parrot owners get caught in a loop where they don't introduce their parrots to new things because the parrot is scared of them and the parrot is scared of new things because it isn't regularly introduced to them. It is imperative not to get into this kind of situation. At the same time, it is also important not to introduce new objects to a frightened parrot in a way that will make it scared of being introduced to new objects in the future. In other words, going "cold turkey" on a scared parrot and forcing it into a new cage, changing its toys, or making another big change can reinforce its fears of novelty and only make things worse in the future.

The key to relieving a parrot's fears is to give it the freedom to overcome them on its own. If the parrot feels forced into a situation it cannot control, it will already be scared preemptively regardless of how harmless it is. On the flip side, without some intervention on your part, the phobic parrot will entirely avoid even trying the things it is scared of. This is where the training process plays a phenomenal role. And the great thing is that the more times you use it, the easier it will be to desensitize a parrot to new things in the future.

Your target stick is your friend. Since from the very beginning the target stick has brought no harm to the parrot and only good things (like treats and safety), the parrot is likely to trust the target stick. It can also serve to distract the parrot from its fears by focusing the bird on a goal. To begin the introduction of a new object – it could be a new training prop, toy, perch, or just about anything – start with some target training without the object being in sight. Target the parrot around on a table or on the floor a few times to remind it about targeting. Always give treats when the parrot touches the target stick. Slowly unveil the new object or place it at a good distance from the parrot. Don't pay any attention to the object but continue targeting the parrot around the area where you originally started. Since the object is playing no role in targeting and is not affecting the parrot, the bird should continue to focus on the training. If the parrot is so distracted by the object that it cannot focus on training, put the object even farther away or behind something to keep it out of direct sight. Continue targeting your parrot around the surface in random patterns. Sometimes target the parrot toward the object and sometimes away from it. Don't keep targeting your parrot to the object (unless your parrot is much at ease), but ignore the object and just focus on targeting. By not forcing the object onto the parrot, the object gets to play a smaller role of importance and therefore is less scary.

Use this technique for introducing new objects to your parrot even if it is not scared of them or not expected to be. You may not have to do this with every single object, but it is good to occasionally practice this technique on objects that your parrot would consider entirely benign. The reason is that it helps your parrot develop trust in this process of introduction. If the bird felt at ease getting introduced to dozens of less scary objects, it will trust the process on an absolutely terrifying object some time down the line.

In the same or multiple sessions, continue targeting your parrot into closer and closer range of the novel object but without placing too much importance on the object itself. Do not touch or handle the object. Especially do not move the object closer to the parrot. Instead, continue to encourage the parrot to come closer to the object on its own by using the targeting process. If you target too close to the object that the parrot refuses to come, step back a bit and don't target so close next time. When the parrot gets engaged in the targeting process, continue sneaking the target stick just slightly closer as progress is made. You can also mix in practicing some known tricks in the vicinity of the object to put the parrot in a more training oriented mood. Even though the parrot is not touching or interacting with the new object in this process, it is receiving treats and feeling safe.

As you continue getting your parrot to target in the immediate vicinity of the object, begin placing your free hand on the object, slowly moving it, rotating, and manipulating it so that your parrot becomes fearless of the object from all angles. This also ensures that the parrot is not scared of you bringing the object up to it. As a final step, instead of targeting the parrot to the object, bring the object up to your parrot (but still give treats for the parrot allowing the object to come close or touch it). At this point the parrot is no longer fearful of the object and you can use it as a training prop, hang it in the bird's cage, or go about using it in the manner it is meant to be used.

This socialization process makes a parrot at ease around new objects more readily down the line. Eventually, after introducing dozens or even hundreds of different things using this method, your parrot will look forward to seeing new objects (to have the opportunity to earn treats). Since in every prior exposure to new objects, the parrot was treated with exceptional care (treats, attention, and safety), the parrot will welcome new objects simply out of habit. The long term product of this process is a parrot that is happy to accept new objects without any fear.

Introducing People

The process for introducing parrots to other people is similar to introducing new objects. However, the most principle difference is that people, unlike objects, can behave and respond in their own way. The introduction of other people becomes as much, if not more, about training the people than the parrot.

Simply put, people are clueless about how to behave around birds. Some are terrified, others don't realize the potential danger. Some people treat them like a puppy and others think they are no smarter than a fish. Since you as the owner are educated and familiar with parrot handling while your guests are not, it is imperative that you guide the entire situation for a positive outcome (for people and parrot alike). If your parrot bites another person, this can be very bad. Not only is it a shame that someone gets hurt (although sometimes after provoking a bird they really had it coming), but it also reinforces your parrot to bite other people in the future. Like with biting in general, prevention and training are key to making your parrot behave well around others.

It is really important to use good socialization techniques whenever other people are to interact with your parrot no matter how difficult or easygoing your parrot is. Even if your parrot never bit anyone before, the last thing you need is for it to pick up a habit of biting from one instance of poor handling. Just because someone tells you they own parrots or have experience means nothing either. Even if they are exquisite parrot handlers (which most often is not the case), no one knows your bird like you do. This is why it is imperative to use the following approach for all people that your parrot is not already familiar with. By consistently using the socialization approach, your parrot will pick up on the familiarity and apply prior success to new people much more quickly.

Socialization is crucial for companion parrots because if not for what we teach them, they're wild birds. All too often a parrot will bond to its caretaker or someone in the family and then be aggressive toward everyone else. If you think about it, this makes sense. The parrot gets everything it needs/wants from this individual while everyone else is erratic, unpredictable, and possibly dangerous.

Guests, visitors, and strangers are possibly the worst people from the parrot's perspective. At worst, they come and invade their territory, scare them, and make them feel helpless. At best, they leave them alone while diverting their owner's attention away from the parrot. Either way, there is nothing to be gained by the parrot and everything to be lost so it's not a wonder parrots typically don't like company. This is why socialization through a positive reinforcement approach is so important. Here I will outline the steps I take with my birds and suggest you follow with yours when introducing any new people.

First, never take the parrot's tameness for granted. Just because it steps up for you and doesn't bite (if it does, you're going to have to go back to basics before introducing others) does not in any way mean that it will behave this way towards strangers. Hopefully, the parrot has a history of training and positive reinforcement from you, which gives it a reason to be around you. Or perhaps, it's just used to you and nothing else. Regardless, don't take this for granted and invite others to handle your bird straight away because most likely this will result in failure, bites, and – worst of all – encourage your parrot to be aggressive towards people.

Here are my 12 steps toward introducing people and having a well socialized parrot that will step up for any person:

1) Ignore the bird. Have your visitor ignore the bird. The worst thing that could happen is your visitor gets excited that you have a parrot and goes straight to the parrot cage upon entry. The parrot doesn't know what to think of this and chooses to get defensive, rather than waiting to see what happens. Even if the parrot doesn't get a chance to attack your guest, it will still develop a bad first impression that this individual is potentially dangerous. So instead, it is best to pretend the parrot doesn't even exist for the first 10-60 minutes.

The visitor should avoid eye contact or walking straight toward the parrot. The guest should just go about things as though you didn't have a parrot at all. I usually tell people that I'll show them the parrot later but for now we'll do something else. This shows the parrot that the guest is harmless and avoids setting a bad impression. This gives the parrot a chance to the watch the guest within the safety of its cage without feeling trapped by an approaching stranger.

2) Let the bird loose. Let the parrot out of the cage and let it choose whether to approach or not at its own pace. Again, don't allow the visitor to impose upon the parrot. Ideally, the parrot should be flighted and given the chance to fly closer or retreat at its own comfort level. Most likely the bird will approach out of curiosity or come to you for security. Letting the parrot – rather than the guest – set the pace, guarantees the bird will not be overwhelmed.

3) Show how to handle the parrot. You must realize that most people have never handled a parrot before and don't know how to. Even the ones that have, still don't necessarily know how to handle your parrot, so assume you must start from scratch with anyone. If your guests learn to handle the bird as you do, it will be more familiar for the parrot. Show your visitor how you approach the bird, how it steps up, how you pet it, etc. Don't give people the opportunity to treat your bird like a dog or a child. They have to understand that this is an intelligent free willed animal deserving respect and admiration.

4) Human perch. Let your visitor's first contact with the bird be as nothing more than a human perch. Guide your visitor to hold their arm or finger out to accept the bird and do nothing else. NEVER let them just reach in and have the bird step up. You can't be sure what they will do nor what the bird will do. Many times this will result in a nasty bite, but if nothing else, will assure the bird that it's safest to just avoid strangers all together. You parrot should already be familiar with targeting beforehand (Chapter 4), so you should be able to target the parrot onto your visitor's hand and then back off. Again, remember that the first time on someone's hand should be uninvolved. The person should not pet or handle the parrot yet. Showing the parrot that it can stand on random people's hands without anything happening is far more reassuring than something unpredictable going on.

    Hold the visitor's hand or arm to ensure stability, especially with children. You don't want them to drop their hand under the weight of the bird stepping on. Use your hands to keep the parrot's attention and deflect a potential bite. Don't give an opportunity to either visitor or parrot to get scared. If one gets scared, the other is sure to become scared too. A scared, biting parrot will make a human scared; by the same token, an unsure human will scare the parrot into biting.

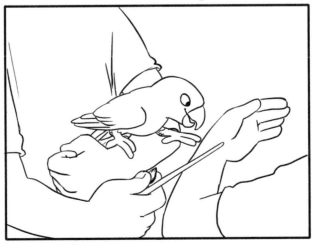

5) Tricks. The bird should be trick trained beforehand. This is yet another reason why trick training is so useful. Have your visitor cue tricks from your parrot and reward it with treats. This is fun and exciting both to visitor and parrot. Allow the visitor to present bigger treats or the best ones you save for special occasions. This will help the parrot overcome the unfamiliarity and even look forward to visitors instead of dreading them. This is a fun, safe, hands off approach to use positive reinforcement with the parrot for socialization.

6) Step Up. Only after going through the prior steps do you actually allow a new person to request the parrot to step up. What you did was build a certain level of trust in the bird before having someone actually move their own hand toward it. By the time you think it's appropriate for a visitor to approach the bird for step up, the bird has received good things and nothing bad so it's worth a try. My preferred way for having my parrots step up for visitors is by surrounding the bird with tricks. My parrots are accustomed to receiving treats after performing a trick. Thus I have the visitor cue a trick, then while approaching with the treat, ask the parrot to step up to get it. The parrot already knows it earned a treat, so it might as well step up to get it. This gives the parrot less reason to doubt motives. After a few successful step ups as such I switch it around. I have the visitor get the bird to step up first for the opportunity to preform a trick for a treat. Thus, the parrot learns to simply step up to earn potential opportunities and not exclusively when a treat is in the hand. Again, it's good to go through these stages with your parrot yourself before completing them with visitors so that the parrot knows what to expect.

7) **Petting.** Now that the parrot is comfortable being on hands, we can introduce hands for petting. Remember that people don't know how to handle or pet a parrot, so you must show them the way your bird likes it. This is not a time for experimental petting. If your bird won't end up liking it, then it will avoid allowing people to do it in case it's bad like that again. I have my parrot stay on my hand and hold its beak between my fingers. This teaches it a submissive pose, puts a buffer between biting guests, and tells the bird what's about to ensue. I begin by scratching my bird's neck the way it likes and then having the guest reach in and join together. Then, I take my hand away and allow them to continue. Since the parrot was enjoying it from the start and the visitor did nothing more than continue it, the parrot allows it and even enjoys it. This creates a reason for the parrot to look forward to visitors and not dread that they will manhandle it in some terrifying way.

8) **Bird Potato.** Play bird potato with one or more guests by randomly passing the parrot around between people and handling it. Mix tricks, scratches, step ups, and taking breaks randomly so the parrot becomes accustomed to as many people and hands as possible but always keeping it desirable for the parrot.

9) **Grab training.** Teaching the bird to allow itself to be grabbed by different people is not only useful when that needs to be done (grooming, vet, boarding, emergency, etc) but it also builds a greater level of trust. If the bird will trust someone to grab it and not bite, then it will especially feel safe and not bite just standing on their hand. At first, this process may take days or weeks, so it is good to work with someone

familiar. Eventually, the more people you follow these steps with, the easier and quicker it will go. Have the visitor come as close to the bird as it allows and give a treat. Then the visitor should progressively bring the hand closer to the bird without touching and then give a treat. Eventually, the visitor should be able to touch the bird for a treat, cup it, and finally grab it for a treat. In the long term, have visitors grab and carry the bird to other parts of the room, grab it on/off the cage, and give treats at mixed intervals. The parrot will become accustomed to being handled by people as a normal activity.

Repeat the above steps with as many people as possible at home. Once the bird is OK with at least a few people, you can begin trying the next approaches.

10) Private Outings. Bring the parrot on private outings with not too many people. Take the parrot to dinner with family, over to a friend's house, etc. Start with smaller events that can be controlled before going to things that are more bustling. These are great opportunities for the parrots not only to meet new people but also to become more at ease with people they already know. This is a good opportunity to continue the socialization process and mend bridges. People that were previously enemies can become friends in unfamiliar places.

11) Public Outings. Once the parrot is used to some people and places, you can begin taking it on outings to public places. Parks, malls, streets, carnivals, etc. are all great opportunities for your parrots to learn that people are harmless and good. Inevitably, people will want to handle your parrot and they will be willing to listen and do as you say. This is your chance to guide the interaction as you have done at home and ensure that interactions with other people will always be good. Since the parrot is busy taking in all the activity of being outside and not within its own territory, it will be less likely to protest. Since humans have always been a safe thing before and the new unfamiliar ones are being presented in familiar ways, the parrot will cooperate. Again, it is your responsibility to ensure that the parrot does not bite or scare people and vice versa. However, successful public outings like this will make your parrot infinitely more robust and social towards people and changes in its life.

12) Uncontrolled Random Interactions. It's inevitable that at some point or another, someone will handle your parrot not in ways that you would recommend. When such interaction happens with an unsocialized parrot, this can set things back. However, once you have accomplished all the previous steps, random interactions can strengthen your parrot's socialization skills. As long as it is not harmful, allow people to handle your bird in random unpredictable ways. Let people be themselves and let the parrot get used to unguided interaction. The parrot will realize that this is harmless and get over it. If you always shelter your parrot, then of course, these unpredictable interactions will be terrifying. But once your parrot is already well socialized, allowing some of these to slip by now and then just makes the parrot more robust and prepared to deal with things you could never have foreseen to prepare it for.

Remember that every person is different and that every interaction will make your parrot more social. At first, control the interactions very closely to ensure that they aren't too much for the parrot. But over time, challenge your parrot with tougher less predictable situations. Even when you achieve a socialized parrot, continue to maintain this over time or it will again become too comfortable with you and not with others. Encourage interaction with family members, friends, and strangers that is always positive to the parrot but also always fun/safe for humans. Don't give humans the opportunity to scare the bird but also don't give parrots the opportunity to bite people and make them afraid of birds either.

Going Outside

One of the most comprehensive forms of socialization comes in the form of taking your parrot outside. Your parrot will be exposed to an infinite number of sights, sounds, smells, and unpredictable situations. This will prepare your parrot better than anything for the time you have to take it to unfamiliar places or introduce major lifestyle changes. Taking your parrot outdoors and/or to public places exposes it to countless people. The more people your parrot has good experiences with, the more trusting it will be of any stranger in the future.

Not only is taking your parrot outdoors the best socialization, it is also essential for its health and well-being. Parrots should receive a minimum of 15 minutes of direct natural sunlight per week. This is the least that it should get, but more time outdoors is better. Your first outdoor introductions should be kept short and simple. Even if you intend to take your parrot out wearing a harness, take it outside in a carrier for the first few times. You were introduced to getting your parrot used to the carrier in Chapter 5. Make sure the parrot has been sufficiently exposed to the carrier prior to taking it out in it for the first time.

For parrots that are unaccustomed to being outdoors, wait for a day when the temperature is similar to indoors (+/− 10°F is fine). For most species, once your parrot is used to going out, the temperature range can be up to +/−20°F from household temperature or in the range of 50°F-90°F. At the lower temperatures, seek direct sun and avoid windy conditions. At the upper temperatures, avoid direct sunlight and seek shade.

Scout out a more serene location where you can take your parrot outdoors near your home for the first time. If you have a backyard, that may be best. Set out a chair and sit with your parrot in its carrier. By no means should you leave your parrot outside on its own. Your first outings should not be longer than 15-30 minutes. Over time, you can increase this duration up to all day if you'd like. As long as the weather is suitable, even a complete homebody parrot can become acclimated over time.

Although outdoor aviaries are a great way for parrots to spend time outdoors and play, they serve less benefit to the quality of the human-bird relationship so they are no substitute for personal outings. A combination of both is ideal. But if choosing only one, stick to the personal outings instead.

While at first you are seeking less hectic places to take your parrot outside, over time you want to challenge your parrot by taking it to more public places. After the backyard, a session in the front yard will expose the parrot to new things such as cars and passerbys. In these earlier outings, as tempting as it may be to show off your parrot, leave it be and don't allow people to come up and check the bird out. To make outings more desirable, you can sprinkle food or treats in the carrier for your bird to enjoy while out. It is possible and even likely that your parrot will be too captivated by the situation to bother eating. This is OK, but you want to keep practicing these in-carrier outings until the parrot is accustomed enough that it is at ease enough to eat treats.

Do not take a parrot outside unrestrained whether it is clipped or not! No matter how exquisite of a flier your parrot is indoors, do not think this will suffice outdoors. There are too many distractions, factors, and dangers outside to merit putting your parrot in this sort of risk. No matter how clipped and sedate your parrot is, do not think this will keep it safe outdoors either! There are all too many cases of clipped parrots getting carried off by wind. But don't think the risk is just a parrot flying off. There have been cases when parrots merely jumped down to the ground and were hit by a car, snatched by a dog, or stolen by another person. For a common pet parrot, these risks are simply too great and not worth taking. A carrier, aviary, or harness are the only methods of restraint that can ensure your parrot's safety to the maximum extent possible. There are still risks and dangers to all of these that are beyond the scope of this book. Be fully aware of the dangers and do your best to mitigate them.

Before taking your parrot outside with a harness as the safety restraint, make sure the following requisites have been practiced to a good extent: step up, handling/grabbing, flight recall, harness donning, harness removal, and spending time in harness. Outside is the last place you want to be learning that your parrot won't let you grab it or that it knows how to undo its harness. It is very important that your parrot is tame and easy for you to handle indoors before taking it out. There could potentially be situations where your bird lands somewhere dangerous or gets tangled and requires you to handle it in different ways to resolve things. Be sure to review Chapter 6 and make sure your parrot is harness-comfortable before going out. Make absolutely sure the harness is securely clipped to your belt loop and <u>not</u> on your wrist.

It is really important not to use a harness as a primary means of controlling your parrot outdoors. It is only there in case your parrot gets spooked and reflexively tries to fly off while ensuring the parrot cannot fly too far. However, the main thing keeping your parrot from flying away or ensuring it will come back to you must be your training relationship. If you aren't 90% confident that you could safely take your parrot outside and home without a harness (but still choose not to because the risk of complete loss is not worth it), then you shouldn't do this using a harness. Stick to a secure carrier or don't take your parrot outside at all until you develop those skills. The reason I make an allowance for a 10% uncertainty is because it is necessary to start taking your parrot outside wearing a harness and training it in the outdoor environment to build up the remaining certainty.

While the first few times you take your parrot outside wearing a harness are riskier due to its inexperience, there are things you can do to reduce the danger. As previously mentioned, having practiced all behavior at home to a satisfactory extent, having taken the parrot out in a carrier multiple times, and having had the parrot practice wearing the harness at home are an important start. On your very first harness outing, put the parrot's harness on inside the house and proceed out. As you open the door, cup the parrot against you to prevent any sort of startle as the door opens. There could be a stray/wild animal, person, or something unexpected beyond the door and you don't want your parrot's first seconds outdoors to end in panic.

Take your parrot someplace near, preferably a place it is already familiar with. Continue holding your parrot close. This both prevents your parrot from bailing and provides it a sense of security/familiarity. By preventing the parrot from having a fly-off early on, you are teaching your parrot to stay put while wearing a harness. Work on slowly loosening your grip and eventually transfer your parrot to stand on your hand. Grip the leash so that the parrot cannot move anywhere except walking on your hand. Hover your other hand over the bird to ensure this and to provide security cover. If your parrot tries to take flight, you should be ready to catch and cup it to calm it. Giving the parrot a chance to fly off won't make it feel safer like it might indoors because it will soon hit the end of the leash and be unprepared to deal with it. Once you note your parrot is beginning to relax, you can reduce your level of intervention. Slowly give the parrot more walking room by holding the leash with more slack for your parrot.

The more uneventful outdoor harness situations you can have with your parrot where it does not fly off, the better. It's much easier to later teach outdoor harness flight than it is to convince a terrified parrot – that hit the end of the leash, fell on the floor, and got hurt on its first day out – to trust being outside. Keep giving your parrot more and more slack on the leash as you make progress. Find a safe place for your parrot to perch. Ensure that there is nothing else within the radius of the leash for the parrot to get tangled on should it take off. Give treats to your parrot to make being outside while wearing a harness more pleasant. When your parrot becomes well-relaxed, practice targeting or tricks to keep it occupied and earning treats.

Once you've experienced this success in one location, repeat the same process in new locations. Don't assume that your parrot won't try to fly off in a new location just because it didn't in a prior one. Use the same caution when exposing your parrot to new places until enough experience is built up that you know the bird is OK going anywhere. Remember that whatever you allow your parrot to do early on is more likely to stick. So don't let your parrot perch on places you don't want it to but do allow it to perch where it can. In the earlier stage, keep the parrot on you the majority of the time so it can always revert to you for safety. Do not allow the parrot on your shoulder until extensive harness success is achieved. There is a greater chance of a take off or a bite out of fear when the parrot is on your shoulder. Keeping the parrot on your hand for at least the first dozen outings will give you more time to react and keep your bird safe.

Sooner or later there will be a situation when your parrot takes off and hits the end of the leash. It is best to prepare the bird for this, to the extent possible, by practicing short flight recalls. As the parrot becomes more used to flying outdoors and to you, it will be more likely to fly back to you after a fly-off. This will happen sooner or later, but it is important to physically prevent this from happening too early on and sully the entire experience of being outdoors or wearing a harness. After a few times hitting the end of the leash, the bird will either learn to turn and come back to you or learn to avoid taking off. Reflex may still take over (perhaps a car blowing a tire nearby) but will at least be reserved only for the most frightening situations.

As you and your parrot become more experienced at going outside together, the sky is the limit. But, only as long as it's not further than the end of the leash. You'll be able to walk around your neighborhood with your parrot or drive places in your car (preferably keeping the bird in a carrier and then donning the harness before stepping outside). As your parrot becomes more used to being outdoors, you'll be able to baby it less and less. It wasn't long before I could walk down a bustling street carnival with children screaming and balloons popping with my parrot on my shoulder and almost forget she is there. Continue challenging your parrot by having it meet people, visit new places, and be exposed to novel unforeseen situations.

Taking Trips

Bringing your parrot on trips is not only fun or practical, but is also some of the best life preparation for the bird. Owners run into major problems with their parrot when they need to move to a new home or rehome the bird. Since the parrot has never been out of the house before, this ends up being a very traumatic experience for the bird. The best way to prepare for any such situation in the future is to take your parrot to lots of different places early on. When your parrot has been exposed to many different locations, moving to a new home will be no big deal at all.

Another great reason for taking parrots on domestic trips with you is because leaving the bird home (or boarding the bird) may be difficult or undesirable. When you take the parrot with you, you'll be able to take good care and bond with it. At home parrots can become too accustomed to routine and even sport bad habits. When they are out, they are more likely to bond with you, other family members, and other birds in your flock.

Be sure to research pet friendly hotels or (if the weather is suitable) you can camp with your parrot. Be sure to use extra precautions when keeping a parrot loose in a tent and that the tent is never opened until the parrot is put away.

Taking the parrot to other people's houses is great too. However, be sure to pay more attention to safety. Just because you have taken great precautions to bird proof your own home, does not mean the home you are visiting is safe. Watch out for Teflon/PTFE cookware, open windows, single outside doors, ceiling fans, pest traps, other pets, and other hazards you have learned to protect your parrot from. Sometimes, someone else's living room is too dangerous to let the bird out. Keep the parrot in the carrier in those areas and find a small safe bedroom to give the parrot a bit of time to stretch its wings.

Car trips, walks, and even air flights are all great ways to take your parrot around with you. Each is an experience in itself and makes your parrot more well rounded. A parrot that has been there and done that will be far more receptive to change, new people, new things, less stressed, and easier all around to keep. Next time you are planning a family vacation, try to keep your feathered companion in mind and incorporate it into the plans.

Boarding

While on the subject of travel, inevitably some trips will just be unsuitable for bringing a parrot. For these, you will need to either have someone come over to take care of your parrot at home or board your parrot elsewhere. Either way, the best way to prepare your parrot for this is to take it places and intentionally not take it places throughout its life. In other words when you go out on weekends, sometimes bring the parrot but other times leave it at home. If the parrot is both used to being out but also used to staying home alone, it will be best prepared for in home or out of home boarding as needed. It is best to prepare it for both because if at the last minute no one you know can take care of the bird, you may be forced to board it elsewhere.

The order of preference for care of your parrot in your absence is:

1. Parrot stays home in its own cage and someone comes daily to take care of it
2. The parrot is brought with its cage or carrier to stay with someone you trust
3. The parrot is boarded at a veterinarian or pet care facility

If your parrot is well rounded and not spoiled for attention, leaving it home is best. If the parrot is brought to stay with someone else (or boarded), then not only are you gone but the place is all different too. If the parrot is left at home, then at least it has one familiar thing for comfort in your absence.

You must be careful about who you have take care of your parrot in your absence. Don't let anyone convince you they know what they are doing just because they have many pets or even parrots. Make sure you go over everything the way you do it and don't assume they know how to take care of your bird. If the temporary bird care taker is afraid of the parrot or the parrot is terribly aggressive toward others or you just don't trust them to have the bird out, teach them to change food, water, and papers from outside the cage only and not let the parrot out. A few days or even a week without out of cage time is not terribly detrimental as long as the parrot is properly fed, watered, cage cleaned, and provided with an abundance of toys. If you have already practiced this sort of solitude previously, your parrot should be able to deal with it just fine (refer to Plucking section in Chapter 8). It is best to switch to a freefeed pellet diet while someone else cares for your parrot. Discontinue the feeding schedule and provide food in abundance in case the caretaker misses a session or there are any issues. If your parrot is good about eating its pellets, discontinue fresh foods to make things simpler and reduce risk of spoilage. A week or two on pellets alone and freefeed won't substantially impact your parrot's health as long as you return to your normal feeding routine when you are back.

Chapter 9 Checklist:

☐ Socialization prepares parrots for future life changes
☐ Introduce new objects, people, and places to socialize
☐ Use target training to desensitize parrot to new objects
☐ Introduce new people more gradually, follow 12 steps:
☐ 1) Ignore the bird
☐ 2) Let the bird loose
☐ 3) Show how to handle parrot
☐ 4) Human perch
☐ 5) Tricks
☐ 6) Step up
☐ 7) Petting
☐ 8) Bird potato
☐ 9) Grab training
☐ 10) Private outings
☐ 11) Public outings
☐ 12) Uncontrolled random interactions
☐ Outdoor temperature can be +/−10°F indoor temp initially
☐ Outdoor temperature can be +/−20°F indoor temp eventually
☐ Make first outings in travel cage or carrier
☐ Keep initial outings short
☐ Take care parrot does not fly off during first harness outings
☐ Progressively increase outing durations
☐ Take parrot with you on trips
☐ Leave parrot home with care taker or at a boarding facility

Chapter 10: Lifestyle

Initially, the majority of our attention goes into befriending and taming a parrot. So much energy is spent teaching the bird to step up and be friendly. Soon enough, you may find, that the problem is taking parrot friendliness too far.

When a parrot becomes overly dependent on human companionship, new problems can emerge. Screaming for attention, feather plucking, even biting other people can follow. Developing a well-behaved parrot is not solely about building a connection, it is also about teaching independence. It is all about finding balance. The goal is to have a friendly parrot that can be content to spend time without you as well.

It is never too early to start developing a balanced parrot keeping lifestyle. In addition to your training and relationship building exercises, work on teaching the parrot to stay occupied in your absence. Find and purchase supplies that will help you achieve this.

Toys

Bird toys are great for keeping a parrot busy. But, they need to be the right toys and the parrot needs to learn what to do with them! Do not take for granted that just because it is a bird toy that it will work for your bird.

Not only is it important to provide a substantial quantity of toys, it is also important to provide toys that will keep your parrot engaged. Some parrots are naturally big chewers and will go through any toys you put in front of them. If that is the case, fabulous! You just need to continue providing them in abundance. However, if your parrot is lazy or even if your once-big-chewer parrot loses interest in toys, selection of toys will become a bigger deal.

To begin getting a parrot more interested in toys, start with easier to chew toys. Go one or several sizes smaller than recommended for your size parrot. For a macaw, perhaps try a toy intended for an African grey or even a conure. For a conure, try toys for a lovebird or budgie. Focus more on toys your parrot can chew and break rather than move around. Find toys with less plastic and more things that the parrot can actually break. Thinner wood slices, popsicle sticks, paper, and natural materials are the way to go.

Find a toy that you think will be so easy that your parrot will destroy it in five minutes. I promise you it won't be a waste. It is important to build a habit of toy chewing and this is more likely to be accomplished with excessively easy rather than difficult toys. The bird needs to succeed in the kindergarten of toy chewing before going to 1st grade, 2nd grade, etc. The goal is to build a strong background in toy playing before gradually increasing the difficulty level.

While giving your parrot excessively easy toys all the time will keep it busy, the cost won't be easy to keep up with! Gradually provide toys of slightly greater difficulty level. Eventually, the bird will learn to keep busy with toys that will take greater effort and time to destroy.

In some cases, just providing the right toys may be enough. But, oftentimes, parrots would rather play with our toys than with theirs! We humans are poor role models to our pet parrots when it comes to toys. They observe us playing with our phones, remote controls, purses, and keyboards. The problem is that parrots naturally use their beak instead and that wreaks all kinds of havoc on our human toys.

Your parrot likely does not have other parrots to learn to play from, so you must take that role. Sit with your parrot (either in the cage, on tree stand, or on training perch) and hold the five minute super easy bird toy. Run the toy through your hands and find things about the toy to talk about. For example, "look at this amazing toy! It has leather, beads, and wood. This wood is colored red. I like red colored wood!" As you show the toy, start breaking pieces of with your hands or pretend to chew it with your mouth. Do not give the toy to the parrot at first. The more you want the parrot to play with it, the more resistant the bird will be. Instead, show the bird how much you like it. When the parrot is just boiling with jealousy and is dying to try it, finally hold it up to the bird and let the bird break a piece off. Create a routine of playing with your bird with bird toys on a daily basis. This will help your parrot grow more accustomed to engaging with toys regularly.

Even when you are not directly working with your bird (but within sight), try to let the bird see you more involved with bird toys rather than human ones. Instead of holding the remote while watching TV, fiddle a bird toy between your fingers. Don't let your parrot see you texting on your phone, but instead do let the parrot see you holding a bird toy while reading a book. Simply put, let your bird see less of what you would rather it not do and more of what you would rather see it do. Bird toys are cheaper and safer than keyboards, phones, and purses for the bird to destroy!

Parrots seem to care more about materials, shapes, and textures of toys rather than appearance. Try to choose toys that will be more engaging rather than necessarily based on how nice they look. Natural toys that sport an assortment of natural materials tend to be safer and more engaging than highly colored toys, particularly plastic or acrylic ones. Remember that parrots primarily play with toys by breaking them. Don't try buying toys that the parrot cannot break to save money. It is the process of breaking toys that keeps a parrot engaged and quiet, whereas indestructible toys tend to lose a parrot's interest quickly and remain unused.

Foraging toys can be used as an additional incentive for parrots to play with toys. Particularly, seek destructible foraging toys that you can hide treats inside of. Indestructible foraging toys are OK from time to time, however, they do not do a good job of teaching a parrot to be more involved with toys in general. Destructible foraging toys on the other hand, give the parrot practice in toy destruction and help create independent play routines. Over time, you can use smaller and fewer treats in the foraging toys, but the parrot will continue destroying toys out of habit.

Continue building interest and involvement with parrot toys both inside the cage and out. Practice the habits you would like to become routine. Over time, you may become less involved in playing with bird toys but the habit will stick with your parrot. A busy beak is a quiet one!

Parrot stands

Don't expect to be able to just put your parrot down on a bare empty bird stand and go about your business. If the parrot gets bored, it will find its own ways to keep busy. Unfortunately, the ways the parrot will naturally find to stay busy are not compatible with the well-behaved parrot or house pet philosophy! At minimum, the parrot will chew up the perch you set it on. Worse yet, the parrot may choose to fly off and find some furniture to chew. If that isn't an option, then it may revert to screaming for your attention.

As you learned, prevention is key. You need to prevent bad behavior in order to promote good behavior instead. Always ensure that there is something keeping the parrot busy whenever it is out.

The first way to keep a parrot engaged while out of the cage is by providing direct attention from you. This can be in the form of training with treats. While the parrot is interested in earning treats from you, it will stay where you are doing the training. You can also provide engaging attention such as talking or playing with toys together.

However, it is not possible to provide one-on-one attention all the time. You may be able to keep the parrot busy by having it out while there is something for the parrot to watch. Perhaps you or someone else is involved in a hands-on activity that provides the parrot something to focus on. However, if you are in a sedate environment engaged in a passive activity such as reading or on your phone, it is difficult to expect the parrot not to get bored. Either put the parrot away in the cage before it can get into trouble and learn naughty behavior, or provide acceptable things for the parrot to do.

You can use an array of different perches and play stands to give your parrot a variety of activities. Furthermore, these will serve to get the parrot into a certain mood at each different place. Parrot stands not only serve as "bird furniture," but they can also help your parrot find its place in the home environment. A tree stand, training perch, tabletop perch, window perch, and shower perch all have their own place and function. The Parrot Wizard online store offers an extensive collection of patented NU Perch® stands for each of these purposes. Since they all look similar but fill different purposes, it is easy to get a parrot to get comfortable and learn its role on each one. You can browse and read more at https://ParrotWizard.com/Trees

Tabletop Perch

A tabletop perch is a great way to set your parrot down without having your parrot on the furniture. It has is portable and has a base that can catch your parrot's. You can take it from room to room with you.

For potty training and behavioral reasons, you should not have your parrot on you for more than short lengths of time. At minimum, you need to set your parrot down periodically to poop. To avoid the parrot getting nippy or too shoulder drawn, use a tabletop perch to set your parrot down anywhere you go.

Unlike a tree stand, a tabletop perch is plain and barren. There aren't toys or various levels to climb around on. And, unlike a training perch, the height isn't particularly suitable for focused training either. You cannot simply set a parrot on a tabletop and then focus on your own tasks. The perch itself is too plain and boring to keep a parrot from misbehaving for long.

The best use for a tabletop perch is when you will be doing some sort of physical activity that will be amusing for the parrot to watch. For example, folding laundry, changing light bulbs, assembling furniture are active tasks that will draw your parrot's attention. You can add even more excitement by talking or singing in the process.

Over time, the parrot will learn that a tabletop perch is like a seat in a theater! A good place to calmly watch what others are doing. Use the tabletop perch wisely and it will be a useful tool in your well-behaved parrot toolkit.

Training Perch

Training perches are best used for just that, training. Whether you get a manufactured Training Perch™ or designate a specific perch or chair back, you should reserve your training perch only for training.

From an early age, children learn the different purpose of different chairs. A chair at the kitchen table is for eating, a couch by the TV is for watching, and a chair in school is for learning. Likewise, your parrot can learn how to behave on different parrot stands. A training perch is the school chair. When used consistently, just being placed on the training perch will stimulate the parrot to pay attention and focus on learning. Be sure to set the height appropriately and use the training perch strictly for training on a regular basis.

Window Perch

A window perch can be a perch that hangs from a window with suction cups or even just a standing perch by the window. As the name implies, the purpose of this stand is for the bird to look at what is going on outside. Let the outside world entertain your parrot at this station.

Shower Perch

Like a window perch, a shower perch can mount on suction cups or be free standing. This perch can either be used for showering your parrot or for your parrot to keep you company in the shower. Whether or not the parrot gets wet should depend on the bird's personality and if it enjoys participating in the shower. However, just like sitting by the window, watching you soaping up and singing shower tunes can be another way to teach your parrot to stay put while being entertained.

Tree Stand

A tree stand is a parrot's cage away from cage. This is the grand living room for your bird. It can provide climbing, feeding, and playing opportunities for your parrot while away from the cage. Keep in mind that a bare tree stand is no better than other perches. A tree stand is a platform for you to fill out and personalize for your parrot. Just like the cage, it should be filled with ropes, swings, perches, and lots of toys.

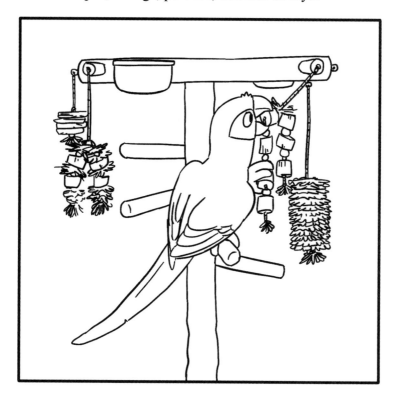

Unlike the previously mentioned perches – where you or something going on has to entertain the parrot – a tree stand is supposed to help your parrot keep itself occupied. But, just like with toys, you may need to spend some effort at first to build this habit (photo page 297).

While it is OK to feed small amounts of food to the parrot on a tree stand, I do not recommend feeding entire meals there. In order to ensure that the bird maintains a good incentive to return to the cage voluntarily, it is best to leave feeding meals to inside the cage. You can use the food bowls on a tree stand for foot toys, dropped toy pieces, and for foraging opportunities. You can fill the food dishes with things to play with and hide treats in between.

Like with toys, it is important to create a play routine with your parrot. You can use targeting to encourage your parrot to climb around the entire stand rather than perch on top exclusively. Whenever you set your parrot on the tree stand, put your parrot on the lowest perch as they will usually climb to the top. Create a routine time for your parrot to play on the tree stand. Participate in this routine in the beginning. Eventually, you will be able to leave your parrot occupied on the tree stand while you attend to passive activities that would be boring for your parrot to watch.

Unlike a cage, the tree stand does not force your parrot to stay there. Only engagement with toys, the practiced routine, and attention from you can convince the parrot to stay on the tree instead of roaming the house. Build these habits strong and build them early. That is how you can use a variety of "bird furniture" not only to provide your parrot with a comfortable place to perch, but also how you can use it to shape good-behavior. You can use this collection of stands around your home or in one room. As you build up an assortment of "bird furniture," your parrot may learn to use its wings to move about between them. If you take the time to develop habits on how to use these stands, the bird will know what to do.

Using the Parrot Wizard Lifestyle, your parrot will have places to go in your home that it will like even better than human furniture. It will help limit the bird's inevitable mess to easy-to-clean stands. By giving the bird places to go, you will help preserve human furniture to be used for humans.

Use the lifestyle approach to find a balanced harmony with your pet bird. Develop a close friendship, but also encourage freedom and independent play as well. Incorporate the Parrot Lifestyle approach as the final step of sharing your home and developing the well-behaved parrot.

Chapter 10 Checklist:

☐ Balance bird-human relationship and independent play
☐ Do not let parrot become too needy
☐ Use toys to encourage quiet independent play time
☐ Choose easy-to-break toys to start
☐ Make sure your parrot is very playful with easy toys first
☐ Gradually choose more difficult toys while maintaining the bird's interest in spending a lot of time on bird toys
☐ Teach the bird how to play with bird toys
☐ Make playing with toys with the bird part of your routine
☐ Do not let the bird see you playing with "human toys"
☐ Fidget bird toys in your hand when your bird is watching
☐ Use foraging toys to teach bird to play with toys
☐ Use parrot stands as "bird furniture" around your home
☐ Each stand has a different purpose based on how it's used
☐ Never leave bored parrot without something to stay occupied
☐ Use tabletop perch for parrot to watch you doing something
☐ Training perches should be used exclusively for training
☐ A window perch is for looking outside
☐ Take your bird in the shower using a shower perch
☐ Outfit tree stand to keep parrot engaged in independent play
☐ Play with parrot on tree stand to build routine
☐ Use Lifestyle approach to building balanced relationship

Conclusion

As you begin to apply taming, training, flight, socialization, talking, outings, healthy feeding, lifestyle and other elements of good care, you will begin to see your parrot shape up to be a well-behaved parrot. It's not simply a matter of any single element but genuinely the culmination of this entire ownership process. With love, dedication, regularity, and patience you will slowly begin to see it reciprocate back. The parrot will greet you when you come home, come to the front of the cage to be let out, unhesitatingly step up on your hand, do its business in an appropriate place, play with toys, spend time with you, accept and even eagerly anticipate head scratches, step up for strangers, allow itself to be grabbed, fly to you on command, travel with you outdoors, and allow you to put it back in its cage. In the span of doing all this, the parrot will not bite, will scream less than otherwise, and will be less likely to develop into a plucker in the long run.

Having read this book, you have come a long way. Now it is time to actually apply this knowledge and make a difference. Reading and becoming aware is one thing, but actually applying it is what it's all about. Be patient; it is only a matter of time. You will be surprised how easily and directly some of these things apply, while at other times you will be stumped because your parrot doesn't seem to fit the norm. It is only in the actual process of working with your parrot that you will personally learn your parrot and your parrot will learn you. You will develop a unique relationship that exists only between you and that very bird. You will have something priceless to treasure and your parrot will too. Hang on tight because a well-behaved parrot is coming your way!

Glossary

Beaking – When a parrot uses its beak as a hand to feel or hold on without malicious intent. Should not be confused with biting which is meant to cause harm. Young parrots are particularly prone to beaking and this natural behavior must be allowed to run its course but should not be reinforced.

Behavior – Observable things that the parrot does. Behavior can be innate or learned. Owners strive to teach parrots acceptable behavior for living in the household environment.

Biting – When the parrot intentionally or reflexively uses its beak to do harm to another being. Biting should not be confused with beaking or nipping which are less painful and without malintent. Biting can happen out of fear, jealousy, self-defense, aggression, hormones, or to get something.

Bridge – Usually a sound that marks a desired behavior to connect the gap between the moment of the behavior and the moment reinforcement is received. A bridge is particularly useful for remote training when an immediate reward cannot be delivered. A clicker is the most common bridge device but saying "good" or showing a treat could also serve as a bridge.

Clicker – A plastic box with a flexible metal sheet that can be pressed to make a click sound. Clickers are useful for marking the moment a parrot displays a desired behavior for which a treat is coming.

Clicker Conditioning – A process of teaching the parrot that the click sound means a treat is coming. By clicking and giving a treat a few dozen times, it allows the bird to make the connection that the click sound leads to a treat. This is helpful when the clicker is used as a bridge to mark desired behavior.

Clipping Wings – Cutting the tips of a parrot's primary wing feathers to inhibit flight. The primary purpose of clipping wings is to serve as punishment for attempted flight by making it more difficult or impossible. This discourages a parrot from attempting flight again.

Desensitization – A process of exposing a parrot – in tolerable doses – to people, places, or objects that it fears in order to diminish the fear.

Extinction – The elimination of behavior by lack of reinforcement. It is desirable for unpleasant behavior to go extinct by avoiding reinforcement. On the other hand, it is necessary to continue reinforcing pleasant behavior to prevent it from extinction.

Eye Pinning – When a parrot's pupils rapidly contract. This is a display of excitement which can either be good or signal an impending bite. Eye pinning happens the same in either case and must be analyzed in context to foresee resulting behavior.

Flight – A natural ability of most birds and parrots. Flight is the primary means of motion and exercise for parrots. Keep in mind that parrots are not born knowing how to fly. They learn how by attempting it. Parrots that had their wings trimmed before they could fledge as a baby, do not know how to fly.

Freefeed – When food is available to a parrot at all times. Even if just pellets are available, it is still freefeed because the parrot has access to food at any time.

Grooming – The process of trimming a parrot's beak or talons to be less sharp. Sometimes may refer to cutting wing feathers as well. Taming and training help ensure that a parrot will be cooperative during grooming and not traumatized.

Healthy Feeding – The combination of what you feed and how you feed it. It is not only important to feed quality nutritious food, but also to make sure it is fed in the right amount and only during scheduled feedings.

Hormonal Behavior – Typically reproductive based behavior triggered by excessive food, changes in daylight, changes in humidity, excessive touching, and other environmental changes. It can include mating rituals, wing drooping, regurgitation, and other unusual behavior. Hormonal behavior must not be encouraged because it can cause aggression, egg laying, and other problematic or unhealthy behaviors.

Lifestyle – The combination of routine, schedule, and environment that improves the parrot keeping experience. "Bird furniture" gives the parrot places to go in your home and advises the parrot how to behave at that location.

Motivation – The parrot's willingness and likelihood to participate in behavior you solicit. Motivated parrots learn new behaviors more easily and quickly. They also continue to exhibit learned behavior more readily. Following the healthy feeding schedule helps improve motivation for training.

Negative Punishment – Withholding or taking something away to reduce a behavior.

Negative Reinforcement – Removing or reducing something undesirable to increase a behavior.

Nipping – An intentional but not hard bite done with the purpose of manipulation and not self defense. Some parrots nip when they want something from you. It is important to prevent and ignore nips or they will become more frequent.

Petting – The process of stroking a parrot's feathers. Parrots like to have their head and neck feathers stroked away (toward their beak, not body). Parrots should be taught acceptable petting seeking behavior and not to bite during it.

Plucking – When a parrot pulls/harms its feathers. This should not be confused with molting when a parrot naturally loses some feathers for replacement. Plucking can be behavioral, clinical, or environmental. See an avian veterinarian.

Positive Punishment – Doing something to the parrot that reduces a behavior. The behavior must actually become less frequent for it to be punishment. Unfortunately most punishment can result in fear from a parrot which will cause it to flee or bite so positive punishment turns out to be ineffective for most training.

Positive Reinforcement – Doing something that increases behavior. Usually giving treats or attention is positively reinforcing and the parrot does more of what earned it the treats. Positive reinforcement is not inherently "positive" as in "good." Positive reinforcement is simply something that increases behavior. Only context can determine whether it is actually good or not.

Potty Training – The process of encouraging a parrot to hold in its excrement and let it loose in a designated place or at a designated time. This is effective for short term but a parrot will still have to go frequently.

Prevention – The most effective means of dealing with problematic behavior. Preventing it from occurring in the first place ensures that it can't be learned and reinforced.

Rehome – When a parrot is transferred from one owner to another for personal reasons.

Rescue – A rescue parrot is one that is transferred for reasons pertaining to the parrot and not the owner. A parrot rescue deals in rescue parrots.

Shouldering – Putting a parrot on your shoulder or allowing it to climb there on its own. It is important to ensure that a parrot is tame and steps up reliably before allowing it on your shoulder. Otherwise biting or other problems may ensue.

Socialization – The process of introducing a parrot to people, places, and objects to make them more tolerable to the parrot. The parrot can be socialized by bringing people and objects into the home as well as by taking the parrot outdoors to come in contact with them elsewhere.

Step Up – When a parrot steps onto a finger or arm. Parrots generally step forward and up. Place your hand to the side of the parrot and give it the chance to choose to come or not.

Taming – The process of reducing response behavior so that you can handle your parrot more.

Target Training – The process of teaching a parrot to follow and touch a target stick to receive a treat. This skill is helpful for teaching a parrot to step up, tricks, and to become comfortable around new objects or people.

Training – The process of teaching desirable behavior and tricks to a parrot for reinforcement.

Treat – A food that is desired by the parrot which leads to positive reinforcement (increase of behavior).

Vocalization – When a parrot repeats sounds it has heard elsewhere. Talking, whistling, and chirping (like other birds) are examples of vocalizations.

Well-Behaved Parrot – A parrot that has learned to cooperate and coexist with people to live in the household environment as a desirable pet. This is the foundation for everything else you may personally wish to do with your companion parrot.

On Becoming the Parrot Wizard

Parrots are my passion! From early childhood, I had a fascination with anything that flies. Birds, planes, and insects would catch my attention.

During my college years, I began learning to fly airplanes and was searching for my first pet. A pet bird was without doubt my best match! I briefly had a cockatiel named Spock. Unfortunately, he was short lived, but he ignited a spark that would become my passion with parrots. He made me realize how little I know about parrots and inspired me to learn all that I can. Spock paved the way for Kili and becoming the Parrot Wizard.

With Kili, my Senegal parrot, I discovered an aptitude for trick training. I realized that through trick training, we were strengthening our bond while having fun. I began sharing these tricks and experiences on YouTube and thus the Parrot Wizard channel was born.

I soon added Truman, a Cape parrot, to the mix. His name was inspired by the movie "The Truman Show," because "While the world he inhabits is, in some respects, counterfeit, there's nothing fake about Truman himself. No scripts. No cue cards. It isn't always Shakespeare, but it's genuine. It's a life." ~Christof. From day one, Truman was supposed to grow up to be a big star. I documented everything from his arrival to every trick he learned. Yet, Truman saw his role differently.

It wasn't until Truman accidentally flew away that I realized he wanted a different life for himself, not in the spotlight. Truman's rebellious excursion around New York City made my heart sink and I feel eternally grateful for getting him back. Not only did Truman alter my role for him, he also led me to meeting Marianna.

Marianna also had a lifelong passion for birds. She had Rachel, a blue and gold macaw, before we ever met. I soon discovered that we had more in common than an interest in parrots and we got married.

Truman found his purpose in life with Marianna as a cute, cuddly, chatty, house-pet and they are now best buddies. This is the story of how I ended up with my current 3 parrots, Kili, Truman, and Rachel.

Along the way, I adopted Santina, a green-winged macaw, from a parrot rescue. It was amazing how much trust we built in a matter of weeks using taming and training. This was a chance to rehabilitate an older parrot and demonstrate how effectively parrots can be trained regardless of their background. In the span of a week I taught her to voluntarily wear an Aviator Harness and offer a DVD sharing these sessions. Santina now lives with Lori near Pittsburgh and is the sweetheart of her life. I am thrilled that I was able to rehabilitate and prepare Santina for her awesome new home.

I have had the pleasure of participating in TV Shows and events all around the world. Whether it was the Steve Harvey show or a weekend long seminar presentation in the Czech Republic, I have been blessed with opportunities to share my love and knowledge of parrots.

During my appearance on the Late Show with David Letterman, Mr. Letterman concluded, "you are wasting your time in the computer business, my friend." He inspired me to go into the parrot business full time. Since then, I founded the Parrot Wizard company, wrote my first book, patented my NU Perch®, designed innovative parrot behavioral supplies, released hundreds of videos, and toured the world giving parrot presentations.

While my personal experience ranges from training a budgie to a macaw, my proudest achievement is the success of my students. Through my books, videos, webinars, seminars, and events around the world, I have had the opportunity to bring people and their parrots closer together. I value their feedback and am always fine-tuning my presentation.

I am pleased to take all I have taught and learned over the years and bring you the most comprehensive parrot keeping approach in this second edition of the Parrot Wizard's Guide.

Photos

Michael with trained parrots Kili, Truman, & Rachel

Grabbing parrot out of carrier for first time

Healthy feeding is the basis of a healthy relationship

Provide an abundance of toys to keep the beak happy & quiet

Set Training Perch height so parrot's head is below your chin

Single Handed Target *– Hold clicker, target, and treat*

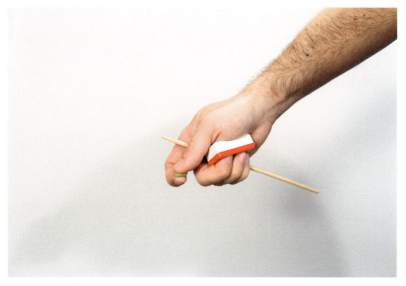

Eventually make target stick appear shorter to phase it out

Target parrot onto handheld perch from the side

Hold finger, hand, or arm across handheld perch

Target parrot onto hand without holding a perch

Target parrot to come off of shoulder

Hand taming by hovering hand above parrot

Teach voluntary nail grooming

Teach your parrots tricks for fun and improved behavior

Outfit your Parrot Lifestyle with trees, stands, and toys

Voluntary hold and grab training

Roll parrot on back by holding...

...and rolling back. Release feet and hold parrot on back.

Use two Training Perches for flight recall training

Target parrot to fly between stands and then to your hand

Flight is beautiful and a highlight of having a pet bird!

Always clip harness leash to belt loop, even indoors

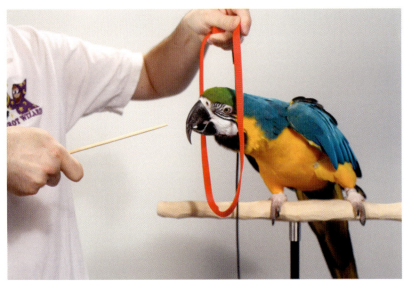
Target parrot to reach into spacious "fake collar"

Target parrot to stick its head into real collar of harness

All harnessed up and ready to go outside safely

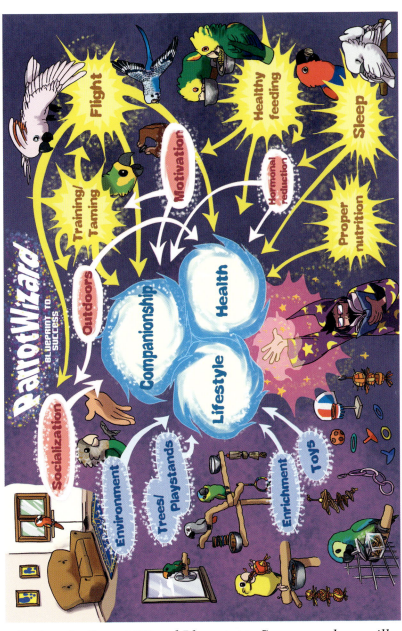

Follow the Parrot Wizard Blueprint to Success and you will discover how amazing a well-behaved parrot can be!

Appendix A: Further Reading (and Videos)

Teaching Tricks

How to Teach a Parrot to Wave http://TrainedParrot.com/Wave

Teach a Parrot to Fetch Objects http://TrainedParrot.com/Fetch

Teach a Parrot to Shake Head http://TrainedParrot.com/Shake

Teaching to Hang Upside Down http://TrainedParrot.com/Bat

Making Parrot Show its Wings http://TrainedParrot.com/Wings

Teach Go Through Tube http://TrainedParrot.com/Tube

Teaching Turn Around http://TrainedParrot.com/Turn_Around

Flight Related

Joy of Flight http://TrainedParrot.com/Flying_Parrots

Flight Safety http://TrainedParrot.com/Flight_Safety

Flighted Fetch http://TrainedParrot.com/Flighted_Fetch

Indoor Freeflight Training in a Large Gym
http://TrainedParrot.com/Gym

Putting a Harness on a Cape Parrot
http://TrainedParrot.com/Cape_Harness

University Lecture About Evolution of Flight
http://TrainedParrot.com/Evolution_Of_Flight

Training & Behavior

Basics of Taming a Parrot http://TrainedParrot.com/Taming

Treat Selection For Training http://TrainedParrot.com/Treats

Training Motivation http://TrainedParrot.com/Motivation

Challenging a Parrot http://TrainedParrot.com/Good_Behavior

Put Parrot Back in Cage http://TrainedParrot.com/Caging

Toweling Parrot Training http://TrainedParrot.com/Toweling

Advanced Clicker http://TrainedParrot.com/Clicker_Method

Outings & Socialization

Parrot Socialization http://TrainedParrot.com/Socialization

Taking Parrots Camping http://TrainedParrot.com/Camping

Parrots at Carnival http://TrainedParrot.com/Carnival

Miscellaneous

Emergencies http://TrainedParrot.com/Disaster_Preparation

Introducing New Foods http://TrainedParrot.com/New_Foods

Parrots Out in Winter http://TrainedParrot.com/Winter_Parrots

Ginger's Parrots Rescue for Senegal Parrots
http://TrainedParrot.com/Gingersparrots

Continuous vs Variable Ratio Reinforcement Ratios
http://theparrotforum.com/viewtopic.php?f=15&t=1439

Ginger's Parrots Rescue, a non-profit rescue in Arizona, employs the approach outlined in the Parrot Wizard's Guide to Well-Behaved Parrots on the rescue Senegal parrots housed there. The rescue strives to rehabilitate the parrots to be healthy, friendly, and ready for being reintroduced for adoption as a desirable family pet. Please support the outstanding efforts of this rescue by sending supplies or a money donation to:

http://GingersParrots.org
Contact@GingersParrots.org
480-382-5411

Appendix B: Useful Products

Parrot Training Perches

http://TrainingPerch.com

These stands are essential for parrot training! They provide a distraction-free environment for focused training. Adjust the height for your comfort either standing up or sitting down. Add an optional Potty Tray. Available in sizes for every parrot. Made and sold exclusively by the Parrot Wizard.

Clicker & Target Stick

http://ParrotWizard.com/Clicker_Target

Pick up a clicker and target stick set to help you start parrot training. Extra clickers, clicker 3 pack, and clicker/target stick set available from Parrot Wizard.

NU Perch

http://NUPerch.com

Parrot Wizard's patented NU Perch is the most comfortable perch your parrot has ever set foot on! Textured, bumpy, comfortable, stylish, completely safe, these wooden perches feature all stainless steel hardware. Available in an assortment of sizes. This is the ultimate parrot perch.

Woodland Parrot Toys

http://WoodlandParrot.com

Woodland Parrot is a series of artisan parrot toys embodying nature, happiness, and design. Surround your parrot with exciting woodland creations that bring harmony and pleasure to your feathered companion. Natural materials, safety, comfort, and that special allure that will keep your bird engaged are at the soul of these toys. Hand made in USA.

NU Perch Scale

http://ParrotWizard.com/Scale

Scale with a comfortable and familiar NU Perch for quick and easy weighing of your parrot on a daily basis.

Aviator Harness

http://ParrotWizard.com/Harness

All companion parrots taken outdoors should either be in a solid carrier or wearing a harness. The Aviator Harness is by far the easiest and most comfortable of the harnesses available. Without any buckles, it's simply a matter of pulling a few straps to tighten.

Toys

http://ParrotWizard.com/Toys

Check out the abundant selection of exciting parrot toys offered by Parrot Wizard. You will love these toys because your parrot will love them! Keep that beak happy, quiet, and engaged.

Nail Trimmer Stone

http://ParrotWizard.com/Nail_Trimmer

Keep those nails trimmed to save your hands from those sharp claws and keep your parrot from getting caught on things. Using positive reinforcement you can train your parrot to participate voluntarily in the nail trimming process safely.

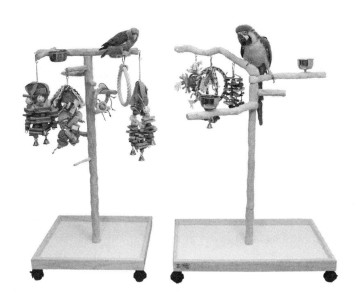

NU Perch Trees & Stands

http://ParrotWizard.com/Trees

Parrot Wizard offers an entire range of parrot trees and stands to help you provide an engaging environment for your parrot. This serves as a complete line of "bird furniture" that is so appealing to parrots, it helps keep them off of your human furniture. Furthermore, every stand serves a unique purpose to help improve your parrot's behavior. Use a Tabletop Perch for spending time with your parrot, a Training Perch for training, a Scale Perch for weighing, a Window Perch for looking outside, and a Tree stand for independent out of cage time. Learn more about how to use Parrot Wizard trees and stands to improve your parrot's behavior and lifestyle at http://ParrotWizard.com/Lifestyle

Index of Photos & Illustrations

The Parrot Wizard's Guide, Front Cover

Well-Behaved Parrot, 4
Parrot Wizard Blueprint to Success, 16
"Parrot Shopping", 19
Cost of Owning a Parrot, 27
"Getting Comfy", 49
Household Hazards to Parrots, 56
First Meeting, 62
"Training", 79
Effective Training Setup, 83
Quit While You're Ahead, 86
Test Motivation, 90
Using a Clicker, 97
Single Handed Targeting, 106
Target Large Parrot onto Handheld Perch, 107
Target Medium Parrot onto Handheld Perch, 109
Target Medium Parrot onto Perch/Hand Transition, 110
Target Large Parrot onto Perch/Arm Transition, 111
Picking Up Small Parrot, 112
Picking Up Medium Parrot, 113
Picking Up Large Parrot, 114
Hand Taming, 117
How Not to Hold a Parrot, 121
Turning Parrot on Back, 125

"Good Behavior Management", 127
Petting Etiquette, 135
Target Parrot Off Shoulder, 139
"Taking Flight", 152
Teaching a Parrot to Fly With Training Perches, 157
Harness Training, 171
"Trick Training", 176
Teaching Turn Around, 184
Teaching Go Through Tube, 186
Parrot Fetching, 189
Teaching Fetch, 191
Teaching Basketball, 192
Parrot Talking, 194
"Resolving Problems", 203
"Socialization", 240
Desensitization Training, 244
Step Up for Other People, 250
"Keep Busy", 266
Tabletop Perch, 273
Tree Stand, 275
Parrot Lifestyle, 277
Author With His Harnessed Parrots, 280
Parrot Wizard, 289
The End, 319
Michael & Kili, 320

Loving Relationship With Parrot, Back Cover

Color Photos

Michael with Kili, Truman, and Rachel, 290
Grab Out of Carrier First Time, 291
Healthy Feeding, 291
Abundance of Toys, 292
Training Perch Height, 292
Single Handed Target, 293
Phase Out Target Stick, 293
Step Up on Handheld Perch, 294
Step Up on Perch/Arm Transition, 294
Step Up onto Hand, 295
Step Off Shoulder, 295
Hover Hand Taming, 296
Nail Grooming Training, 296
Basketball Trick, 297
Parrot Tree, 297
Grab Parrot, 298
Turn Parrot on Back, 299
Flight Training, 300
Flight Recall, 301
Clip Harness to Belt Loop, 302
"Fake Collar" Harness Training, 302
Real Collar Harness Training, 303
Wearing Harness, 303
Parrot Wizard Blueprint to Success (Color), 304

Index

African grey 28, 30, **33**, 75
Amazon 30, **33**, 75
basketball 188-192
biting **205-216**
    displaced **201-210**
    excitement **211**
    fear **205-207**, 239, 241
    jealous 24, **210**, 281
    learned **212-215**
    possessive **207-210,** 239
    territorial 208-209, 225-226
    hormonal 212-213, **224-228**, 283
boarding **263-264**
boomerang 162-163
breeder 37-47, 67, 74-75, 153
bridge 95-96, 281-282
budgerigar 28, **31-32**, 34, 68-69, 92, 188, 268
cage 12, 22, 31, 45, **50-55**, 58-59, 64-66, 71-75, 82, 88-90, 106-107, 116
    putting parrot into/out of **129-132**
    time **149-150**
caique 30, 32-33

capturing 187, 196, **199-201**
carrier 12, 26, 28, 53, 58-59, **143-146**, 173, 255-258, 262-263
claws 146-149
clicker **95-99**, 105, 177, 281-282
clipping wings 23, 40-42, 44, 55, 149, 153-157, 166, 204, 235, 257, 282
cockatiel 25, 28, 31-31, 68-69, 92, 188, 287
cookware 28, 56-57, 262
conure 30, 32, 188
cost 22, 26-29, 31, 268
cue 130, 142, 158-159, 165, 177-178, **180-190**, 196-197, 200-201, 251
desensitization **72-74,** 205, 243, 282
diet 17, 26, 41, **67-68**, 76, 92-94, 213, 220
fetch 163-164, **188-193**
flight 17, 23, 44, **152-175**, 204, 206-208, 221, 235-238
grab **115-121**
grooming 121, 146-149, 283

harness **165-174**, 255, 257-261
health 14-17, 29, **46-47**, 67-69, **92-94**, 132-133, 143, 220-221
hormonal
    behavior 17, 230, 283
    biting 212-213, **224-228**, 283
lovebird 30-32, 268
macaw 22, 30, 75, 120, 268, 288
motivation 17, 69, **89-92**, 132-133, 179, 226-227, 283
nipping 138-140, 211-212, 284
nutrition 15, **67-68**, 92-93, 148, 226, 283
outside/outdoors 17, 155, 160, 165-167, 173-174, 231, 241, **254-262**
parakeet 22, 30-31, 69, 105
parrot *passim*
parrotlet 30-32, 34, 188
petting 14, 119, **134-137**, 211, 226, 252, 284
plucking 22, 33-34, 153, 204-205, **220-224**, 234-235
poicephalus 30, 32
positive reinforcement **86-87**, 89, 91, 95, 122, 128, 149, 197, 214, 232, 248, 251, 285
potty training 12, **140-143**, 272, 285

prevention **88-89**, 210, 214, 220, **233-235**, 236, 247, 271, 285
price 22, 26-29, 31, 38-39
rescue 24-25, 30, 37-39, 42-46, 50, 63, 80, 214, 285
retrieve 163-164, **188-193**
screaming 14, 23, 33-34, 54, 90, 149, 153, 197-198, 204-205, **216-220**, 234-235, 267, 271
Senegal parrot 32, 188, 287, 307
shouldering **137-140**, 234, 260-261, 285
sleep 17, 50, **71-72**, 213, 225
socialization 205, 207, 209, **240-265**, 285
species
    African grey 28, 30, **33**
    Amazon 30, **33**, 75
    budgerigar 28, **31-32**, 34, 68-69, 92, 188, 268
    caique 30, 32-33
    cockatiel 25, 28, 31-31, 68-69, 92, 188, 287
    cockatoo 30-31, 33-34
    conure 30, 32, 188
    lovebird 30-32, 268
    macaw 22, 30, 75, 120, 268, 288
    parakeet 22, 30-31, 69, 105
    parrotlet 30-32, 34, 188

poicephalus 30, 32
Senegal parrot 32, 188, 287, 307
step up 15, 52-53, 71-72, 93, **97-106**, 110, **118-120**, 139, 146-147, 168, 174, 198, 214-217, 223, 238, 241, 244, 257, 277
store 21, 27, 37-40, 43, 45, 47, 53, 63, 74-75, 153
talking 14, 23, 33, 43, 91, **194-201**, 217-218, 286
taming 12, 17, 25, 30-31, 34, 43, 66, 81, 99, 104, **115-125**, 166-169, 247
target
   stick 99-100
   training **99-115**, 113, 138-139, 145, 158-159, 168, 170-173, 178, 183-186, 212, 227, 243, 245, 286
   tricks **183-187**
touch 115-121, 134, 147
toweling 59, **122-123**, 147-148, 181
toy 17, 22, 26-28, 34, **53-54**, 65, 76-77, 89, 91, 94, 131, 208-209, 211-212, 217-218, 222, 233-235, 237-238, 242-243, **267-270**, 275-276
training

flight 106, **141-156**, 172, 174, 184, 223-227
tricks 10, 74-75, 82, 96-97, 105-106, 108, 115, 134, 148-151, **157-174**, 182, 184, 187-188, 191, 193-194, 199-201, 211, 216-217, 225, 231, 241, 244-248, 251, 253, 255, 276-278
treat 53, **69-71**, 73-75, 84, 86, 89-117, 122-125, 128-135, 138-139, 145, 147-148, 159-164, 168-173, 177-179, 186-187, 193, 196-197, 200, 209-210, 216, 230, 245-251, 253, 270, 286
tricks 10, 74-75, 82, 96-97, 105-106, 108, 115, 134, 148-151, **157-174**, 182, 184, 187-188, 191, 193-194, 199-201, 211, 216-217, 225, 231, 241, 244-248, 251, 253, 255, 276-278
   basketball 188-192
   boomerang 162-163
   go through tube **180-182**
   nod 187
   shake 187, 305
   slide 182-183, 186
   turn around 180, 183-185, 305
   wave 180, 182, 187, 305

wings 187, 305
trip **261-264**
tube 180-182
turn around 180, 183-185, 305
variable ratio reinforcement 193, 307
veterinarian 10, 46-47, 53, 68, 93, 143, 220, 222, 224, 263
vocalization 14, 21, **194-201**, 218-220, 223, 286

wave 180, 182, 187, 305
weight 93, 213
   weighing **132-134**
well-behaved 13-18, 27, 29, 34, 39, 45, 68, 76, 80, 88, 91, 92, 115, 125, 140, 147, 155, 193, 201, 216, 222, 224, 228, 241-242, 267, 270, 273, 277, 279-280, 286

Wishing you love and success with your feathered friends!
www.ParrotWizard.com